The New

Ministry of Justice

An Introduction

Bryan Gibson

With a Foreword by **David Faulkner CB**

WATERSIDE PRESS

Acknowledgements

This book could not have been written without the help of many people too numerous to mention, but I am particularly grateful to various regular Waterside Press authors from whom I have gleaned many of the finer points. In the run up to publication I also had various reasons to be grateful to Peter Williams, Alex Gibson, John Lyon and Bob Morris.

As ever, my thanks are due to Waterside Press house editor, Jane Green

I am also grateful to David Faulkner of the Centre for Criminal Justice Research at Oxford University for agreeing to glance over the manuscript and write the Foreword. His knowledge of this aspect of our public institutions and its background goes back over many years and is, I think, quite unrivalled. Some of his own thoughts on a UK Ministry of Justice are contained in his influential work *Crime, State and Citizen: A Field Full of Folk* that I have quoted from in *Chapter 1* of this book. That work contained the germ of what is now a reality. In the outcome David offered more support than I had anticipated and I am indebted to him for this. I must stress, however, that the process of writing this book - and its counterpart *The New Home Office* - took place in a novel context in which not just two but, so it later transpired, several of the UK's major departments of state were being significantly altered. Information, developments and nuances were at times emerging by the day. Any errors that may have resulted from such dynamics remain mine alone.

I must also acknowledge the various sources now available on the internet that I have tried to read, digest and whenever possible reflect upon as they flashed by on my computer screen. Links to some of the more important and useful of these together with other references are noted in *Appendix V* of this work. I would stress, however, that this book is not intended as a detailed or academic work, rather it is no more than is claimed in the sub-title, an introduction – but one in which I have tried to capture something of the democratic, constitutional and justice *zeitgeist* that now appears to be roaming free in and around the headquarters of the new Ministry of Justice in Victoria Street, Westminster.

Bryan Gibson
August 2007

The New

Ministry of Justice

An Introduction

The New Ministry of Justice
An Introduction

Published by
WATERSIDE PRESS
Domum Road
Winchester SO23 9NN
United Kingdom

Telephone 01962 855567 UK Landline low-cost calls 0845 2300 733
E-mail enquiries@watersidepress.co.uk
Online catalogue and bookstore www.watersidepress.co.uk

ISBN 978 1904380 35 1

Cataloguing-In-Publication Data A catalogue record for this book can be obtained from the British Library

Part of a two book set with *The New Home Office: An Introduction*, ISBN 978 1904380 368. The ISBN for the two volumes together is 978 1904380 375.

North American distributor International Specialised Book Services (ISBS), 920 NE 58th Ave, Suite 300, Portland, Oregon, 97213-3786, USA
Telephone 1 800 944 6190 Fax 1 503 280 8832 orders@isbs.com www.isbs.com

The New Ministry of Justice

CONTENTS

CHAPTER

About the author

Bryan Gibson grew up in South Yorkshire before moving to Cambridge, Salisbury, Bristol, London, Basingstoke and Winchester during his legal career. He is a barrister, former co-editor of the weekly legal newspaper *Justice of the Peace* and a regular contributor to that journal and other national media. He founded Waterside Press in 1989 and has since written or edited a number of books for that imprint on aspects of crime and punishment whilst also working on a project to create an *A-Z of Criminal Justice*.

The author of the Foreword

David Faulkner CB was for many years Deputy Under Secretary of State at the Home Office where he worked with no fewer than seven different Home Secretaries, gaining unique insights into and experience of the workings of that department and central government generally. He is now a senior research fellow at the Centre for Criminal Justice Research at Oxford University and a prominent and widely respected commentator on constitutional matters. His writings include the acclaimed *Crime, State and Citizen: A Field Full of Folk* (Second edition, Waterside Press, 2006).

Foreword David Faulkner

The Ministry of Justice (MOJ) was created in a situation where the traditional principles of justice, human rights and the rule of law were under greater pressure than at any time since the Second World War. The main concern was that these principles could not be sustained against the threat of international or fanatically-inspired terrorism of the kind which had been seen in the USA on 11 September 2001 and in London on 7 July 2005. But criticism went further and extended to the perceived failure of the UK's traditional system of justice to protect the public from other dangers of the modern world – the effects of migration, globalisation and the breakdown of family and social relationships. Those effects ranged from anti-social behaviour to sophisticated fraud and organized and international crime, and included new concerns about the threat presented by sexual and violent offenders.

In the UK, the traditional principles of justice are often traced back to the English common law, to Magna Carta, and to the philosophers and jurists of the Enlightenment. They include the presumption of innocence, proportionality, judicial independence, due process and the rule of law. An offender is seen as a person who is empowered by free will, deserving punishment but entitled to dignity and respect as a human being, and capable of change and improvement. After the experiences of fascism and the Second World War, those principles found expression in the European Convention on Human Rights (ECHR), incorporated into UK domestic law by the Human Rights Act 1998.

There is a contrasting view of justice which sees the criminal as someone who is essentially 'different' from 'ordinary' people, of less value as a person, and as a threat from which those holding this view of him or her and the state have to be protected. Justice is the mechanism by which that protection is provided, and the test is a largely pragmatic or utilitarian one: whether things 'work'. From this same perspective, the effect of events on the criminal is of less account than the interests of law-abiding members of society.

Both views have influenced public opinion and public policy to different degrees at different times. They could, more or less, be reconciled in the legislation and practice which prevailed for most of the 20th century, and the need to balance the rights of the individual against the protection of the public has been a consistent theme in the Home Office. The potential for conflict in terms of the uneasy mix of Home Office responsibilities and the way that it may have tended to discharge these - had become more evident in modern times when home secretaries also faced a sometimes hostile media - and the second view has thus become more prominent as criminal justice became more politicised. Neither can changes in society and the world order be discounted. In summary, it may have become more difficult to resolve the conflict between public safety and doing justice within a single department than in the past.

The idea of an MOJ had been debated at intervals since the middle of the 19th century and it featured in the Labour Party's manifesto for the 1992 general election (five years before it came to power). The arguments were based sometimes on efficiency, but more often on the need to reinforce the traditional principles of justice in the absence of a written constitution. But even by 2007 there had been little real consultation before the decision was announced, even though fine traces of the Government's intentions can be found by the more diligent follower of public affairs. Indeed, it came as a surprise to many people, including the judiciary. Some critics believed it marked a shift in the Government's priorities towards what those critics saw as a potentially repressive emphasis on public protection and security; others saw it as an attempt to increase the Government's control over the criminal justice process and as a potential threat to the independence of the judiciary.

From a different perspective, the decision to create an MOJ was seen more positively as one of a series of reforms, perhaps long overdue, designed to improve the quality of justice and to bring the structure of its administration up to the standard required in a complex modern society and a liberal democracy. From this standpoint, it was a logical extension of other changes which the Government had made, or was in the process of making, including the Human Rights Act 1998, the reform of the House of Lords, reform of the office of Lord Chancellor so that he or she no longer has a role in three separate and sometimes opposed arms of state, and the creation of a Supreme Court.

The immediate tasks for the MOJ were to resolve the crisis of overcrowding in prisons and to complete reforms of the National Probation Service already in progress. It is to be hoped that a new ministry, with a closer relationship with the judiciary, might be better able than the Home Office to achieve a satisfactory resolution of a number of long-standing issues in this field. In the longer term, it might also provide the space within which policies on criminal justice could be more dispassionately formulated and reviewed, and from which a more rational, humane and, in the end, more effective response to crime and punishment could emerge. Beyond criminal justice, there is a range of constitutional and other issues to be resolved if Britain is to keep its place as a modern, humane and progressive society. It must be hoped that the new demarcation of responsibilities as between the MOJ and the Home Office will enable the relationship between the state and the individual and the balance between the rights of each to be maintained in accordance with those principles of justice that are part of UK history and identity, of which the nation can continue to be proud.

David Faulkner August 2007

Preface

This book sprang out of a project that I was working on at the time when the new Ministry of Justice (MOJ) was announced in May 2007. This explains why it was possible to turn to writing it so soon, by combining a ready source of information with that about the new regime, which was rapidly coming on stream. The creation of the MOJ and 'slimmed down' Home Office (the commonly used description) - both stem from the same cohort of changes. They represent a step change in public affairs, but one that also draws on developments and thinking that have been taking shape for a number of years. It is a pivotal event, something that is yet more evident when the changes are viewed alongside the restructuring of certain other government departments that took place following a change of prime minister in June 2007. There is also now active discussion of democratic values and the prospect of a *written* constitution. Perhaps there is no better time to set matters down, take stock and make a few observations.

A straightforward account

I hope that as well as providing a basic outline of the MOJ and its component parts, some flavour of the depth and significance of this step change filters through between the lines of the basic outline that follows. *The New Ministry of Justice* can be read on its own or alongside its companion volume, *The New Home Office: An Introduction* that deals with the 'law and order' side of the equation. As with similar books in the Waterside Press introductory series, the chief aim is to provide a basic, accessible and hopefully constructive account that will be of interest to newcomers, students and general readers as well as to those seasoned practitioners or researchers seeking a useful overview. The book looks at the various strands of responsibility that fall within the remit of the MOJ, but against a wider backdrop: matters of justice, constitutional affairs and relationships across the system. Only occasionally and where developments are controversial or more complicated, does the account stray beyond this. At the end of the book, in *Chapter 10*, I have tried to summarise how the changes presage a fresh era and give rise to new challenges.

A logical progression

The changes described are substantial, wide-ranging and often fundamental in their significance. They have an effect on everything from courts, sentencing and penal affairs to constitutional matters, human rights, democracy and freedom of information. They also have an international dimension, not least vis-à-vis the UK's European obligations. At least in part, they also represent something of a logical progression. Thus, e.g. the Constitutional Reform Act 2005 provided for the statutory separating out of the judiciary (judges and magistrates) from the legislature (Parliament) and executive (the government of the day). As part of the same adjustments, the 2005 Act also dealt with reform of the ancient office of Lord Chancellor so that his or her former judicial functions were transferred to the Lord Chief Justice. It also provided for a Supreme Court that is scheduled to 'go live' in 2009; and the Law Lords, the most senior judges, were removed from the legislature, so that they can no longer take part in the day-to-day business of the House of Lords.[1] Connected developments saw a new and independent Judicial Appointments Commission (JAC) designed to ensure transparency in the appointment of judges and a Judicial Complaints Office (JCO). Even the former Lord Chancellor's Department (LCD) became the Department for Constitutional Affairs (DCA), itself overtaken by the MOJ. Such developments are part of a historic thread that runs throughout this book.

Prisons, probation and parole

Central to the 2007 changes was the transfer of responsibility for prisons, probation, parole and associated matters from the Home Office to the MOJ. This triggered a judicial outcry (but little solid political opposition or public controversy). The fact that judges and magistrates are now under the same umbrella as practitioners involved in 'corrections' (as the carrying out of court sentences are often called) remains an issue. It still has to be fully worked out. Related discussion concerning, e.g. the ring-fencing of court budgets and other devices to protect judicial independence – which incoming Lord Chancellor, Jack Straw, has described as his own 'first priority' - may well come to merge with those about constitutional arrangements in general (above). The new, punishment-based responsibilities of the MOJ are dealt with in *Chapter 3*.

Justice needs a Ministry of Justice

Perhaps, for the time being, the final word should go to the (now former) Lord Chancellor, Lord Falconer when, in introducing the MOJ, he gave the reasons behind it and asserted the truism that 'Justice needs a Ministry of Justice':

> ... through the creation of the MOJ, with the bringing together of important parts of the justice system, I believe that we have the best chance for a generation to find the answers to some intractable problems. Working closely with the other key departments, the MOJ provides the opportunity to look at the system as a whole ... Considerable progress has been made over the past ten years, but now the elements are in place to up the pace ... to make a real difference to peoples' lives ... [and] deliver lasting change.

Bryan Gibson August 2007

---

[1] Even if they had wished to do so. The convention has always been against Law Lords taking part in Parliamentary debates except concerning constitutional or judicial issues.

MINISTRY OF JUSTICE (MOJ)

Secretary of State for Justice and Lord Chancellor (and other 'Justice Ministers').
Accountable to Parliament including via the Constitutional Affairs Committee

Key working partners in government include
Home Office
Cabinet Office
Department for Children, Schools and Families
Department for Communities and Local Government

Central agencies
HM Courts Service
The Tribunals Service
HM Prison Service (HMPS)
National Probation Service (NPS)

Concerns include:
Fairness
Consultation
Research
Victims
Witnesses
Social cohesion

Many MOJ aims are discharged via the voluntary sector, private sector and community links

KEY RESPONSIBILITIES

Constitutional Affairs
Human rights
Democratic engagement
Freedom of information

Protecting the judiciary

Criminal policy
Sentencing policy*
Crime reduction

Access to justice
Law-making
Law reform

Administration of the courts, tribunals, prison and probation services

Sponsorship of many MOJ-linked advisory and other bodies
(Appendix II)

*But see the explanation in *Chapter 7*

Independent roles

The Lord Chief Justice and the judiciary (judges and magistrates)

Judicial Office
Judicial Appointments Commission
Office for Judicial Complaints
Judicial Communications Office
Judicial Studies Board

Sentencing Guidelines Council (SGC)
Sentencing Advisory Panel (SAP)

Prisons and Probations Ombudsman
Independent Monitoring Boards
Inspectors

Law Commission

Other 'arms length' functions including a wide range of tribunal work

The Ministry of Justice and its Main Components

Contacting the Ministry of Justice

Ministry of Justice
Selborne House
54 Victoria Street
London
SW1E 6QW
United Kingdom

DX 117000 Selborne House

Telephone: +44 (0) 20 7210 8500

Web-site: www.justice.gov.uk

Ministry of Justice: general queries email:
general.queries@justice.gsi.gov.uk

The MOJ states that it aims to answer all queries (letters, faxes and emails) quickly and clearly - at the most within 15 working days of receipt and that it welcomes any views that people may have about its web-site.

The Ministry of Justice: An Overview

CHAPTER 1

The Ministry of Justice: An Overview

Never perhaps has such a key development in British legal history happened so suddenly as the creation of the Ministry of Justice (MOJ) in 2007.[1] It arrived, *fait accompli*, before a somewhat bemused legal community and general public, courtesy of the Royal Prerogative that allows UK prime ministers at will to configure (or reconfigure) their administrations, which includes creating fresh departments, changing ministerial responsibility and sharing out duties according to what is deemed to be expedient. The trigger for the MOJ announcement was the assertion by the home secretary, Dr. John Reid, just a few months earlier, that the Home Office had become 'not fit for purpose',[2] but it was the logical conclusion of a process of change which had been taking place over a number of years.

The announcement – a major event in itself – was soon followed by a change of prime minister and further related changes. A detectable change of tone accompanied the announcement that the new, incoming Secretary of State for Justice and Lord Chancellor,[3] Jack Straw MP, would be entrusted with a review of key aspects of UK constitutional arrangements. A Green Paper was issued, *The Governance of Britain*[4] – so that not only is there now a new MOJ but a consultation process in which it is charged with examining the use of certain powers, accountability, democratic involvement, rights, justice and constitutional affairs in the UK. This book is an attempt to place these momentous events into perspective, beginning with a straightforward outline of the MOJ.

DELIVERING JUSTICE

The administration of justice is a key task within any society. Many countries have a special department of government dedicated to this end, so as to draw together a range of justice-related functions under one roof. It is often styled 'Department of Justice' or 'Ministry of Justice'. Until now, the UK has avoided this approach, maybe even priding itself on being different and on the intricacies (even

---

[1] The Ministry of Justice was announced on 9 May 2007.

[2] Some further background appears in *Chapter 10* and a companion volume, *The New Home Office*. In reality, the gestation period of the MOJ goes back well beyond this as can be seen from reports of Cabinet Office discussions going back many months: see later in the text.

[3] The dual title for the head of the MOJ. 'Lord Chancellor' has survived attempts to abolish that role and is the shorthand form of description used in this book: see further *Chapter 9*.

[4] Cm 7170.

obscurities) of its idiosyncratic arrangements.[5] Proposals for an MOJ were first put forward in the mid-19th century, when they were answered with the argument that the Lord Chancellor was already a minister of justice in everything but name.

From the mid-1990s onwards, the former Lord Chancellor's Department (LCD) and later, from 2003, its replacement, the Department of Constitutional Affairs (DCA) did develop an increasingly enhanced portfolio and in 2005 a number of related changes were enacted in the Constitutional Reform Act of that year including with regard to the judiciary and the courts as noted in *Chapter 2*. But the real watershed came in 2007 when, simultaneously with a transfer of responsibilities away from the home secretary to the Lord Chancellor and the 'splitting up' of the Home Office, a fully-fledged MOJ emerged: one that exists *in fact* as well as *in name* and that, according to its own express aims is principally concerned with:

- protecting the public;
- reducing re-offending; and
- sense in sentencing.[6]

CORE COMPONENTS OF THE MOJ

On closer scrutiny the work of the MOJ is far more extensive, detailed and in some instances controversial than might appear from the broadly stated and simplistic ends noted in the previous section. Naturally, it has an extensive and fundamental constitutional role that now stands at the centre of reform of democratic engagement, rights and obligations in the UK. The MOJ is expressly committed to openness, transparency and reform. It took over former or lead responsibilities in relation to the:

- Department for Constitutional Affairs (from the DCA itself);
- National Offender Management Service (NOMS) (formerly Home Office);
- Parole Board (formerly Home Office); and
- Office for Criminal Justice Reform (OCJR) (cross-departmental).

As a result, it now draws together various strands of activity under a broad remit that can be labelled 'justice matters' and 'constitutional affairs'. These strands range from duties and responsibilities in relation to courts, judges and magistrates to those concerning such diverse undertakings as prisons, probation, law reform,

---

[5]　Proponents of such idiosyncratic arrangements have often if somewhat perversely sought to justify them on the basis that the UK has no *written* constitution: see *Chapter 6*.

[6]　Ministry of Justice web-site: www.justice.gov.uk

legal aid, freedom of information and constitutional reform, including, critically, in relation to the last of these, matters touching on the independence of the judiciary (*Chapter 2*) and the separation of powers (*Chapter 6*).

The MOJ's duties and responsibilities can be summarised in more extended form as follows:[7]

- working 'trilaterally' with the other departments that make up the central government strands of the Criminal Justice System (CJS), chiefly the Home Office and Office of the Attorney General (see later in this chapter under the heading *Partnership and Shared Responsibility*);
- HM Courts Service (HMCS), that now oversees the administration of all of the civil, family and criminal courts in England and Wales (*Chapter 2*);
- support for the judiciary, including:
  - appointments via the newly created Judicial Appointments Commission (JAC);
  - a Judicial Complaints Office (JCO); and
  - a Judicial Communications Office (all noted in *Chapter 2*);
- the Tribunals Service across the whole of the UK (*Chapter 2*);
- the National Offender Management Service (NOMS), responsible for the commissioning of correctional services and their administration through HM Prison Service (HMPS) and the National Probation Service (NPS) (*Chapter 3*);
- sponsorship of:
  - HM Inspectorates of Prison and Probation (*Chapter 3*);
  - Independent Monitoring Boards (IMBs) (*Chapter 4*);[8]
  - the Parole Board (*Chapter 3*); and
  - the Prisons and Probation Ombudsman (*Chapter 4*)
- legal aid and the more wide-ranging Community Legal Service (CLS), through the Legal Services Commission (LSC) (*Chapter 5*);
- sentencing policy, including sponsorship of:
  - the Sentencing Guidelines Council (SGC); and
  - Sentencing Advisory Panel (SAP) (both *Chapter 7*);
- criminal, civil, family and administrative law (*Chapter 5*);
- sponsorship of the Law Commission (*Chapter 5*);
- hosting the Office for Criminal Justice Reform (OCJR) (*Chapter 8*);
- the Privy Council Secretariat and the Office of the Judicial Committee of the Privy Council (*Chapter 2*); and
- constitutional affairs, including:
  - electoral reform and democratic engagement;
  - civil and human rights;

---

[7] Developed from a list of MOJ responsibilities provided at www.justice.org.

[8] Formerly Boards of Visitors, i.e. visitors to prisons: see further in *Chapter 4*.

—freedom of information; and

—the management of UK constitutional arrangements and relationships including with devolved administrations for Wales, Scotland and Northern Ireland and Crown dependencies (all noted in *Chapter 6*).

Following a change of prime minister and further restructuring of government departments as part of a fresh administration in July 2007, it emerged that the former Home Office responsibility for youth justice would be shared between the newly-created Department for Children, Schools and Families and the MOJ, including in relation to funding and policy vis-à-vis the Youth Justice Board (YJB) (*Chapter 2*). The YJB would be accountable as a non-departmental body (NDPB) to the MOJ but it is envisaged that appointments to the YJB will be made jointly by the two secretaries of state. The administration of the youth courts and related sentencing matters re juvenile or youth offenders, i.e. those below the age of 18 years, fall within the remit of the MOJ. There are also related cross-departmental interests such as anti-social behaviour (ASB), social exclusion, social cohesion and child protection (most of these also touching on the MOJ's responsibilities in relation to the family courts). As with all matters of cross-departmental concern, the role of Cabinet committees is key to any modern-day understanding of the workings of government, including here in particular the Cabinet Committee on Crime and the Criminal Justice System that is mentioned below under the heading *Partnership and Shared Responsibility*. A list of organizations sponsored by the MOJ appears in *Appendix II*.

Bringing together justice-related functions

When the MOJ was first launched, the then Lord Chancellor, Lord Falconer, asserted that it would focus on improving the justice system for the public:

> The justice system is performing significantly better than in the past, but there is still considerable room for improvement … By bringing together courts, prisons and probation services we will have a coherent system looking at the whole life of an offender from conviction to punishment to rehabilitation.

As will be seen in *Chapter 2* it was one aspect of this 'bringing together' that caused a level of controversy, what sections of the media called an 'outcry' from judges and magistrates. It is thus interesting to note at this stage that on his own first day in office following the change of premiership and its accompanying Cabinet re-shuffle,[9] Jack Straw, the incoming Lord Chancellor, declared that his own 'first priority' was the protection of the independence of the judiciary as enshrined in the Constitutional Reform Act 2005. On a more positive note, there has for some years

---

9 Gordon Brown replaced Tony Blair as prime minister on 27 June 2007.

been a great deal of work towards what some commentators have dubbed the 'seamless sentence'; one with some kind of inherent integrity, as where there is a sentence plan or contract with the offender and work inside prisons blends with that which may follow in the community once a prisoner is released.

One existing difficulty in the field of criminal justice is that resources may often have been diverted away from less expensive and – as many people would claim – equally effective community-based approaches to crime and punishment[10] by a combination of the high cost of prison places, an unprecedented rise in the size of the prison population and the constraints placed on constructive work in prisons by prison overcrowding (*Chapter 3*). A coherent system in which planning, budgeting and resources are better linked together and understood at all stages of decision-making ought to lead to improvements in this critical area.

PARTNERSHIP, SHARED TASKS AND OBJECTIVES

As noted under *Core Components of the MOJ* above, the MOJ is part of a trilateral arrangement – or 'special relationship' – with the Home Office and Office of the Attorney-General, whereby common objectives can be pursued. This involves what is sometimes called 'interdependence', i.e. each component of the system has and pursues its own regular duties, responsibilities and objectives, but their achievement depends on the co-operation of others and the interests of all components have to be taken into account so far as broad strategies and ways of achieving them are concerned. There are inevitable inter-departmental implications, both for operational practice and for priorities for public expenditure. Perhaps the most notably overlapping concerns are those affecting the reduction of crime and the prevention of re-offending, which feature prominently as key aims across a number of departments and services. A similar shared approach is sometimes required towards the sponsoring of Bills in Parliament; something that seems to be the intention as between the Home Office and MOJ with regard to public safety or emergency legislation (as noted in the next section). The role of the Lord Chancellor in its changed guise is noted in *Chapter 9*, but it is useful to record here that, according to the MOJ, he or she works:

> with the home secretary, the attorney general and other ministers to ensure flexible and effective responses to different types of crime, from anti-social behaviour to serious and organized criminality ... All three departments will work closely and collaboratively. ... The [three] departments will have a special relationship [and] policy considerations will be shared early and often between departments as policy is developed.

A Cabinet Committee on Crime and the Criminal Justice System (CCCCJS) has been established in 2007 to be chaired by the prime minister. The Lord Chancellor,

---

[10] If not more effective. The 'alternative to custody debate' goes back to the early-1980s.

home secretary and attorney general all sit on this committee. It goes without saying that any such 'special relationship' or cross-departmental involvement must be balanced with competing individual duties and acknowledge constitutional sensitivities, especially in the case of the Lord Chancellor with regard to protecting the independence of the judiciary (see, further, *Chapter2*).

Areas of shared responsibility

Post-creation of the MOJ, the MOJ and not, as previously, the Home Office, will have lead responsibility for criminal law. But is seems that conventional arrangements within Government are envisaged whereby the Home Office, in liaison with the MOJ, can seek to fast-track such legislation where, e.g. there is a need to do so in order to confront terrorism or other immediate threats to public safety. Similarly, the Home Office has indicated that it would expect to be to the fore or to oversee Bills in relation to police procedures, such as those concerning powers of arrest, to search people or property, and of arrest and detention.[11] One statement by the Home Office on its web-site[12] asserts that it will retain the ability to 'quickly propose and implement' new criminal offences in an effort to pursue shared crime reduction strategies and to satisfy the operational requirements of the police or security services. If issues relate both to police procedures and the criminal law – such as the admissibility of evidence obtained by an investigating officer during an interview with a suspect – it is envisaged that there will be joint oversight of Bills by the Home Office and MOJ, using longstanding mechanisms for collective agreement and the opportunities provided by the new Cabinet-based CCCCJS (above),[13] the National Criminal Justice Board and the OCJR. Summing up partnership at this level, the then Lord Chancellor, Lord Falconer noted that:

> Prior to the [MOJ] … government arrangements meant that the vast bulk of expenditure on justice issues was [by] the Home Office, with courts and prosecutors in two very much smaller outposts. Now the MOJ has responsibility for much of the policy which affects what goes on in the courts, and the work of many of the delivery agencies. The MOJ must work closely with the other agencies and departments … most notably the new slimmed down Home Office itself and the police, the attorney general and prosecutors, and social service departments who connect closely with the Family Justice System … In the area of criminal justice, the National Criminal Justice Board will be vital to this … Supported effectively by the Office for Criminal Justice Reform, the NCJB has, in a pragmatic and focused way, driven change in the CJS because of the way it has produced unity amongst the deliverers. We need to see that process developed. We do not want too much bureaucracy. We do want to see better outcomes.

---

[11] As detailed in statutes such as the Police and Criminal Evidence Act 1984 (PACE), Criminal Justice Act 2003 and Serious and Organized Crime and Police Act 2005.

[12] www.homeoffice.gov.uk

[13] Some pronouncements refer to this as a device for reaching 'formal and final agreement'.

In a move that makes for further clarity and appropriateness, sentencing policy[14] also falls to the MOJ. The MOJ will also lead a new collective process (thus far unspecified but, seemingly, including via the CCCCJS, above) to determine whether legislation, offences and changes to the existing sentencing framework accord with the Government's broader criminal justice, sentencing and penal policies. As noted in *Chapter 7*, the Lord Chancellor has now been invested with certain rights, responsibilities and tasks in relation to the Sentencing Guidelines Council (SGC), Sentencing Advisory Panel (SAP) and related research where these were formerly carried out by the home secretary.

Partnerships across the wider justice system and beyond
Partnership, 'working together', or 'multi-agency working' have been a regular feature of public affairs since the 1980s and with an increasing, modern-day, partiality for community or democratic involvement. With the restructuring, renaming and readjusting of various government departments under prime minister Gordon Brown, many new contexts arise in which liaison and communication between the MOJ and other central government departments become essential.[15] Not least amongst these will be developments and communication in relation to youth justice that, as indicated earlier in this chapter, is now shared with the new Department for Children, Schools and Families. But many other partnerships also serve to facilitate modern-day justice processes and underpin their day-to-day operation. By way of example, there are countless voluntary sector organizations that provide services to the courts and the two arms of NOMS, to witnesses, and to victims of crime. Some are of a charitable nature, others offshoots of the private sector or campaign groups. They range from alcohol, drug treatment and gambling projects to refuges for women suffering as a result of domestic violence and support groups for prisoners or secondary victims of crime (the families of those directly affected by it). These groups are sometimes described as part of 'the wider justice family' and even if not involved in the day-to-day provision of services, are frequently consulted about their relevant interests. The democratic and inclusionary stance of the new MOJ suggests that more could be heard of such devices as and when 'community re-awakening' occurs.

JUSTICE: A NEW APPROACH

The direction and ethos of the MOJ can be discerned from its own flagship publications issued as it was launched. The first of these, *Justice: A New Approach*,[16]

---

[14] In the broader, more general, of the two senses of 'sentencing policy' noted in *Chapter 7*.
[15] A communications and liaison task seemingly enhanced by the existence of the Cabinet committee referred to in this section and other similar committees to be announced.
[16] Ministry of Justice (2007).

sets out the aims and objectives of the MOJ and contains various promises and undertakings – akin to what, in business parlance, might be described as a mission statement. Hence, the MOJ, again adopting the royal plural, asserts that, 'We will:

- reduce re-offending and protect the public: by ensuring that the punishment fits the crime; through ensuring that violent and dangerous offenders remain in prison for as long as they remain dangerous; by breaking the cycle of re-offending through increased use of effective community penalties and rehabilitation, by bringing more offenders to justice and enforcing the orders of the court [see, especially, *Chapters 2* and *3*];
- promote justice: by ensuring fair, effective and proportionate ways of resolving disputes, for fighting crime, reducing re-offending and tackling anti-social behaviour; by ensuring that respect for the rule of law underpins our society, our courts and our institutions [*Chapter 6*];
- provide access to justice for all: by making help and advice and financial support available at the point of need and at the earliest stage, especially for the most vulnerable [*Chapter 5*]; by helping people to find their own solutions wherever possible, but where court intervention is necessary, ensuring that court processes are simpler and more transparent [*Chapters 2* and *6*];
- increase confidence in the justice system: by improving understanding of justice; by giving communities a greater role in the delivery of justice; by making the justice system more effective, accessible and accountable; by providing greater support for people going through the system and by encouraging diversity [*Chapter 8*];
- uphold people's human, information and democratic rights: by improving understanding of rights; by demonstrating that rights are not just for lawyers or minority groups but for everyone; by ensuring government departments and public authorities apply the Human Rights Act 1998 with common sense, balancing the rights of individuals with the needs of wider society; by ensuring that government and public authorities adopt a culture of openness through the Freedom of Information Act [*Chapter 6*]; and
- safeguard and modernise our constitution: by ensuring that it is fit for today's society [again *Chapter 6*].'

Promoting justice

Central to its overarching aims, the MOJ also makes the 'super-promise' that it will promote justice, which it views as important if 'we are to provide and protect a fundamental constitutional right of effective access to an impartial court or tribunal … the right to a fair trial, appropriate punishment and deterrence of offenders, payment of debts, liability following accidents, and responsibilities towards children on parental separation'. These are described by the MOJ as core functions of the state itself, the justice system being just one mechanism via which society sets boundaries, including those of acceptable behaviour, of right and wrong:

> It casts the shadow of the law. The knowledge and existence of an effective and accessible justice system ensures … that most rights or contracts are fulfilled and obligations to others respected without the need for legal action or intervention from the state. And it ensures that, when these boundaries are breached, there is a means by which the citizen and the state can seek redress and then see it delivered.

Justice for minorities has been recognised as an important issue for the last 25 years, with concerns relating to law enforcement, sentencing, penal treatment and the ethnic composition of the judiciary and public service. Overall responsibility for race issues was transferred from the Home Office to the Department for Communities and Local Government in 2005, but justice for members of minorities will always be a central tenet of the MOJ. There is also a Cabinet Office and Home Office-led Respect Agenda[17] and there has been much talk of 'community cohesion', 'multiculturalism', or 'restoring British values'.[18] According to the MOJ, the values that it seeks to uphold should be a matter of pride:

> We should be proud of living in a modern, thriving, liberal democracy. The success, prosperity and stability of the United Kingdom rest on the principles of justice and respect for the rule of law being deeply ingrained in our society and in our values. An efficient and effective justice system is essential to the peaceful and effective functioning of society and the economy …

This placing of MOJ responsibilities in a wider, more dynamic context than simply the provision of courts, prisons and probation resources is in line with other facets of the MOJ, including its role in relation to constitutional and democratic engagement, fairness and equality, signalling that 'we must be relentless in making sure that the most marginalised, vulnerable and disadvantaged in society are treated with fairness'. These and other equally vital matters where the MOJ connects to wider societal objectives are touched upon in subsequent chapters.

Increasing public confidence and other intentions of the MOJ

The MOJ also represents a move to increase confidence in the justice system: 'No matter where people come into contact with the justice system, it is vital that the system inspires confidence'. Hence also in this regard, a key priority of the MOJ is 'to ensure that the public see that the delivery of justice is fair, open, accessible and accountable'. The aim is to achieve this by 'ensuring [among other things] that the system delivers outcomes for the public, not the professionals' and that it puts the needs and expectations of the public, especially victims and witnesses 'at the heart of everything [it] does'.

---

[17] That has also featured as a priority of prime ministers: see www.number-10.gov.uk

[18] Britishness is discussed in *Chapter 6* of *The New Home Office* re UK border controls.

It has long been argued by certain criminologists that the CJS is, at least in part, driven by vested interests and the prospect of personal gain or advancement through earnings, profit, promotion, expansion of 'miniature empires' and so on and the same could be said for other aspects of the justice industry.[19] From the first of the two points noted above, this is just one area that the MOJ seeks to tackle as part of its efforts towards making sure that the justice system connects with communities. There is also the question of ensuring that professionals and practitioners connect to the communities that they serve as noted by the then Lord Chancellor, Lord Falconer, before he left office:

> I have the utmost belief in the quality, the integrity and the ability of the courts, and in those who work in them, from the judges onwards: they are all committed to working day after day to deliver justice ... But they know that courts can, and do, appear remote, that people believe the courts don't understand their problems and have no adequate comprehension of some of the issues faced by the communities they are there to serve ... We want the community to view the courts as being effective and relevant to the solution of the problems of crime and anti-social behaviour they face, as well as for family or civil disputes, but we recognise the courts cannot solve these problems alone ... In terms of criminal justice particularly, there is a sense that courts are removed, attitudinally and physically, from the problems faced by communities, and that the courts do not properly appreciate the nature of or the harm caused by some of the crime and anti-social behaviour they are there to help combat ... The MOJ will make the system more open, with the necessary safeguards to protect the vulnerable, and through balancing the rights of the individual with the interests of the community.

Other declared intentions of the MOJ include (paraphrased):

- transforming the public's experience of justice;
- increasing the transparency of the courts (and other bodies);
- increasing the visibility of justice;
- supporting victims and witnesses through the *Witness Charter* and the *Code of Practice for Victims of Crime* (see further *Chapter 8*); and
- increasing confidence through efficient administration and by 'modernising the delivery' of services.

Leadership

Another significant feature of the MOJ stems from its declared intention to grasp the opportunity that arises from new ways of doing things and to capitalise on leadership arrangements via what, in an analogous context, has been described as 'a Government of all the talents':[20]

---

[19] See, e.g. *Crime Control as Industry: Towards Gulags, Western Style* (2000), Christie N, Taylor and Francis Ltd. This connection is that of the author of this book, not the MOJ itself.

[20] Prime minister Gordon Brown as a prelude to announcing his first Cabinet.

We have made real progress in many areas in improving … justice and penal outcomes. The renewal that comes from new leadership allows us to press these improvements much further. According to the *British Crime Survey,* crime is down by 35 per cent and re-offending levels are falling with reductions in adult and youth re-offending levels of around two per cent since 2000. The chances of being a victim of crime are at the lowest for more than 25 years. More offences than ever before are being brought to justice – more than 1.3 million in 2006. During 2005 over two million civil cases and 380,000 family applications were made. There are more than 20,000 new prison places with plans to build 8,000 more by 2012. Legal aid funding of more than £2.1 billion a year is providing some of the most vulnerable in society with access to justice. We must continue to address the issues, firstly, of ensuring we have enough prison places for those whom the courts wish to send to prison; secondly, of ensuring that the courts are sending the right people to prison for the right periods; thirdly, of giving the public the confidence that community penalties are effective; and fourthly, ensuring that the best providers of prisons and of interventions to tackle re-offending are encouraged to come forward. We will follow the MOJ's first announcement on penal policy, by coming forward in the near future with further proposals for making the court – civil, criminal and family – work better for the public.

A SNAPSHPOT OF RESOURCES AND COSTS

At the time when the MOJ was launched the total number of people employed by it was some 77,000 of whom 49,000 belonged to HM Prison Service (HMPS). Court staff comprised a further 20,000 people and there was an MOJ headquarters staff of 4,000. Other agencies, such as, e.g. the Tribunals Service and Public Guardianship Office account for about 4,000 people. Additionally there are some 21,000 National Probation Service (NPS) staff. In terms of what the MOJ terms 'front line delivery' there are, e.g. 595 court houses (comprising 90 Crown Court centres; 360 magistrates' courts; and 226 county courts), 21 central government tribunals, 139 prison establishments and 42 local probation areas. The total MOJ budget is £8.9 billion for 2007/8,[21] all drawn from existing budgets as noted below:

- £4.7 billion from the NOMS budget;
- £2 billion from the legal aid budget;
- £1 billion from the HMCS budget;
- £0.3 billion from the Tribunals Service budget;
- £0.9 billion from other budgets relating to areas of MOJ responsibility.

In addition, the MOJ capital budget for 2007-08 was:

- NOMS: approximately £500m;
- existing investment within the former DCA of £330m.

---

[21] Approximate with various inter-departmental financial transfers yet to be confirmed.

THE CASE FOR A MINISTRY OF JUSTICE

In his book *Crime, State and Citizen: A Field Full of Folk*,[22] under the heading 'A Department of Justice', David Faulkner points out that suggestions for the reform by the creation of a department or ministry of justice have been put forward from time-to-time over many years. He notes, e.g. that eminent commentators such as Sir Leon Radzinowicz and Roger Hood recall 'the protracted debate that took place between 1845 and 1874, with the conclusion that the Lord Chancellor was already the Minister of Justice and no change was needed'. Faulkner also points to other key historical MOJ-related reference points, occasions and events (summarised):

- a revival of interest in the topic that took place in the context of the reconstruction of government following World War I;
- the idea of an MOJ being a recommendation of Lord Haldane's Committee on the machinery of government;[23]
- the Labour Party committing itself to an MOJ in its manifesto for the general election of 1992;
- the Institute of Public Policy Research including such a ministry in proposals in its 2003 paper, *A Written Constitution for the United Kingdom*; and
- the fact that various people and respected bodies from Diana Woodhouse to JUSTICE[24] have drawn attention to the desirability of an MOJ in evidence to the Royal Commission on the House of Lords.

Given this history of debate, reflection and tentative ideas, few people may have anticipated that an MOJ would arise virtually overnight, in 2007, having been flagged up as a future possibility by a Cabinet committee some months earlier, and without further mature debate or wider consultation. Indeed, e.g. in the mid-1980s and indicative of the sensitivities involved, when many court-related matters still lay in the hands of the Home Office, there was a minor political and constitutional hiccup over a far less over-arching issue concerning who should fund and in broad terms oversee magistrates' courts, then mainly resourced by the Home Office, a residue from the days when they were known as 'police courts'. The backlash was a chain of events that led first to the creation of the DCA and, subsequently, certain other key changes of a directly constitutional nature. It also led to pragmatic solutions such as the eventual introduction of a unified and re-styled HM Courts Service (*Chapter 2*).

---

[22] Second edition 2006, Waterside Press.

[23] Together with an independent commission on judicial appointments now reflected in the Judicial Appointments Commission (JAC) established in 2005: *Chapter 2*.

[24] A leading UK-based legal and human rights organization: www.justice.org.uk

Highlighting the arguments

Here then lay the seeds of what many judges, lawyers and commentators might have considered to be a logical progression – discussion leading to the creation of an MOJ. As part of that debate David Faulkner points to some of the main issues as follows:[25]

> Arguments for a department of justice are of different kinds and would produce different results. The first is one of efficiency: the present division of functions between the home secretary, the Lord Chancellor and the attorney-general leads to lack of co-ordination and inefficiency, and the three offices should be combined in a single department. Such a department would have a single system for its information technology, and a structure which would allow for a single minister and a single chief executive to direct the whole of the criminal justice system. This argument may look attractive from a managerial perspective, but it does not stand up to close examination. There are already suggestions that the Home Office is too large, and its work too sensitive, complex and unpredictable, for a single minister, or a single permanent secretary, to give it the attention it needs. Adding more ministers or a second permanent secretary would only increase the problems of communication and co-ordination which this argument seeks to resolve. More seriously, it would combine functions and responsibilities which ought in a liberal democracy to be separated as a matter of principle. Maintaining justice and the control of crime and disorder are separate functions, and the first should never be subordinated to, or seen as an instrument for achieving, the second.

Such tentative and informed views are by no means unique. Even with the creation of the MOJ, many of the underlying issues implicit in the above passage remain to be resolved, not least those affecting the judiciary (*Chapter 2*). Hopefully, in its zeal to move the UK forwards – and maybe driven by the conviction that history may have little to offer, or that experts can serve to over-complicate matters – the Government has not left too many important considerations out of account.

---

[25] *Crime, State and Citizen*, ibid, p. 340.

CHAPTER 2

The Judiciary, Courts Service and Tribunals

CHAPTER 2

The Judiciary, Courts Service and Tribunals

The judiciary – judges and magistrates (as further described below) – and the courts, stands at the heart of all matters of justice. The judiciary operates separately and independently from other MOJ-related services,[1] including via such mechanisms as 'The Concordat' (see under *Judicial Office*, below). The MOJ is responsible for *court administration* as opposed to *judicial decision-making*, through HM Courts Service (HMCS).[2] The MOJ has a legitimate level of input, e.g. in terms of its interest in ensuring that arrangements exist for judicial training and via the Lord Chancellor's statutory role vis-à-vis the Sentencing Guidelines Council (SGC). Analogous arrangements and principles apply concerning tribunals via the Tribunals Service. Tribunal members are sometimes described as carrying out a 'quasi-judicial' function (some tribunal members or chairs are in fact judges). All these items are dealt with at points in this chapter.

Justice-related responsibilities of the MOJ

In terms of pure, directly justice-related responsibilities in the narrow sense of the word 'justice' and geared to the day-to-day dispensing of justice by independent decision-makers, the MOJ's functions centre on a number of supportive, but essentially secondary, roles. These can be summarised as:

- protecting the judiciary;
- consultation, liaison and communication with or between the judiciary including via a Judicial Communications Office (JCO), 'The Concordat' (below) and providing information, research and statistics (*Chapter 8*);
- supporting the judiciary via mechanisms such as:
  - the Judicial Appointments Commission (JAC);
  - the Office for Judicial Complaints (OJC);
  - the Judicial Studies Board (JSB) (all below);
- law-making and penal policy as described in *Chapter 5*;
- sponsorship of:
  - the Sentencing Guidelines Council (SGC);
  - Sentencing Advisory Panel (SAP) (both *Chapter 6*); and
- HMCS which oversees the administration of all of the civil, family and criminal courts in England and Wales (apart from the House of Lords), something that is further explained below.

---

[1] Although the full details remain to be fully worked out: see also *Chapter 10*.
[2] Except re the Law Lords, when administration lies with the Houses of Parliament.

THE JUDICIARY

Ultimately, it is the Lord Chief Justice of the day and other senior judges, not the Lord Chancellor or MOJ officials, who stand between the state and ordinary citizens in terms of protection from abuse of power, or when it is alleged that an individual citizen has failed in his or her responsibilities vis-à-vis the state or other citizens in some area regulated by the law. The situation is regulated by what in constitutional terms is known as the doctrine of the separation of powers, now reinforced by the Constitutional Reform Act 2005 and Human Rights Act 1998. The doctrine holds that the legislature (or Parliament) must operate independently of the executive (or Government of the day) and that the judiciary and supporting legal system should also operate independently of either of the first two and without any particular bias, undue pressure or interference. This is sometimes put another way by saying that there should be no external interference with judicial discretion whether from the public sector, the private sector or elsewhere. That discretion and the judicial mind-set and training via which it is exercised, can be viewed as the cornerstone of all democratic freedoms (see, further *Chapter 6*).[3]

'Judiciary' is a collective or generic term for judges and magistrates at whatever level or seniority. The judiciary comprises:

- the Lord Chief Justice (and a Deputy Lord Chief Justice);
- the Law Lords;
- the Master of the Rolls (head of the Court of Appeal);
- Lords Justices of Appeal (frequently abbreviated to LLJ as in Smith and Jones LLJs);
- High Court judges (often called 'justices', Mr Justice Black or Mrs Justice Green, and signified with a 'J' as in Smith and Jones JJ);
- Crown Court judges who may be circuit judges, recorders (part-time) or assistant recorders;
- Family Court judges of similar ranks to those in the Crown Court;
- district judges and deputy district judges (the latter part-time);[4]
- justices of the peace (JPs) (also known as 'magistrates');
- people in related roles or those with a specific title, e.g. the Recorder of London (usually a circuit judge) or masters of the High Court; and
- coroners (*Chapter 8*).

---

[3] There is also nowadays an important European dimension also noted in *Chapter 6*.
[4] Re civil matters district judges were formerly called 'registrars' or 'county court registrars'; re criminal cases they used to be 'stipendiary magistrates'.

Law Lords, Lords Justices of Appeal and High Court judges are sometimes described as 'the higher judiciary'. The term 'senior judiciary' is frequently used to indicate the topmost judges, such as the Lord Chief Justice, Deputy Lord Chief Justice, Master of the Rolls or Law Lords. The roles of each are briefly outlined within *Appendix III* to this work, *The Courts of Law*.

Protecting the judiciary

Perhaps the single most important argument in favour of an MOJ rests on the need to protect the independence of the judiciary. As already noted in *Chapter 1*, this was also something that Jack Straw, the incoming 2007 Lord Chancellor, himself a trained lawyer,[5] marked out as his 'first priority'. On one view, the very creation of the MOJ can be seen primarily as a response to that priority; whatever else might be added to its responsibilities. As noted in the *Preface* to this work, the Constitutional Reform Act 2005 provided the mechanism for the protection of certain other justice-related functions. The ancient office of Lord Chancellor was until then always a constitutional anomaly before being revised to correspond with modern thinking and European obligations.[6] Now, instead of the Lord Chancellor presiding over the House of Lords from the Woolsack as was formerly the case (and, should he or she choose to do so, sitting as a judge in the highest UK Court, also named the House of Lords), his or her judicial functions will be performed by the Lord Chief Justice, who will also head a new and forthcoming Supreme Court as well as, e.g. continuing to head the pre-existing Sentencing Guidelines Council (SGC) introduced by the Criminal Justice Act 2003 (*Chapter 7*). The Lord Chancellor's former presiding role in the House of Lords proper has been replaced by that of a Speaker (i.e. chair) of the House of Lords akin to the Speaker of the House of Commons. As part of these same developments, the Law Lords (the most senior judges: below) were barred from any active participation in debates or voting in the chamber of the House of Lords. Again, constitutional developments are further described in *Chapter 6*.

Statutory responsibility apart, Lord Chancellor Jack Straw's assertion that protecting the judiciary is his main priority would seem to have been driven by various factors. These include:

- the fact that the Lord Chancellor is, since 2005/6, no longer the voice of the judiciary within the Cabinet – the function of 'speaking for the judiciary' having passed to its most senior judge, the Lord Chief Justice and which is now reinforced by a new mechanism under which the Lord Chief Justice

---

[5] The new MOJ arrangements do not guarantee that future Lord Chancellors will be lawyers. Indeed, a 'mere' elected or 'lay' politician can now be so appointed: *Chapter 9*.

[6] An attempt by the Government to abolish the role and title altogether failed.

can approach Parliament or its Constitutional Affairs Committee (CAC) with his or her concerns and thereby represent the interests of the judges;[7]
- the need to rectify an omission, in that the position of the judiciary was not specifically addressed in the MOJ's early statements about its new role, purpose, aims and objectives; and
- the desire to send out a signal to pacify concern amongst the judiciary concerning the way in which the MOJ was created, pending discussions about constitutional safeguards within the new framework: *Chapter 10.*

The Judicial Office (JO)

The JO is based in the Royal Courts of Justice in The Strand, London. It supports the Lord Chief Justice and senior judiciary in their various and enhanced roles and responsibilities under the Constitutional Reform Act 2005. It also upholds what is known as 'The Concordat', an understanding between the Lord Chief Justice and the Lord Chancellor that was introduced in 2004 and which was summarised by the then Lord Chief Justice, Lord Woolf as follows:

first of all, The Concordat represents a comprehensive guide to the principles which will govern the future relationship between the Government and the judiciary. What was previously uncertain becomes clearly defined, so both sides know what their respective rights and obligations are ... Secondly, the Concordat is universally endorsed by the judiciary as providing essential protection for the independence of the judiciary into the future. In addition, not only has the government signed up to The Concordat, but both the other main political parties have publicly supported it. Commendably, each party has realised that what is at stake - namely, the independence of the judiciary - is of such importance that it should not be made the subject of damaging partisan debate ... Finally, The Concordat does not exclude the Government of the day from involvement with the judicial process, but instead places that involvement on a proper footing.[8]

In order to provide support to the judiciary, the JO comprises three teams: Planning and Governance; Judicial Human Resource Services; and various Private Offices for members of the senior judiciary.

Judicial Communications Office (JCO)

The JCO was created in 2005 to enhance public confidence in judicial office holders in England and Wales. It provides external and internal communications support. It supports all judges, full-time and part-time, together with tribunal members and magistrates in England and Wales.

---

[7] Ironically Lord Philips, Lord Chief Justice indicated that he might do so concerning the creation of the MOJ and did appear before the CAC: see further *Chapter 10.*

[8] Speech to the Lord Mayor of London's dinner for HM Judges, 21 July 2004.

The Office for Judicial Complaints (OJC)

Again, before the 2005 Act there was no transparent and publicly understood system for dealing with judicial complaints and only occasionally, when, e.g. a judge or magistrate was convicted in a criminal court of some offence, did information about what had happened to the culprit in terms of their resignation or an official warning tend to filter into the public domain. Since 2006, the OJC looks into any complaint about the personal conduct of a judge.[9]

The MOJ gives as an example of such misconduct 'the use of insulting, racist or sexist language' and there is clearly scope for yet more serious behaviour. But the OJC *cannot* deal with complaints about an actual judicial decision or about how the judge managed or handled a case. This falls to the ordinary appeal court processes.[10] Complaints can only be considered once the relevant case is closed. Those about a magistrate or judge are made directly to the OJC; although complaints about the former are normally referred, in the first instance, to a local area Advisory Committee.[11] That committee may dismiss a complaint, or part of it, if it fails to meet criteria set out in the Complaints (Magistrates) Rules 2006.[12] If it believes that there may be a case for formal disciplinary action, it will refer the complaint to the OJC. The Lord Chancellor and the Lord Chief Justice will then consider the evidence and decide what action, if any, should be taken.

The Judicial Studies Board (JSB)

The JSB is a national body that provides training and instruction to all full-time and part-time judges in England and Wales concerning the skills necessary in a judge. Historically, it reported to the Lord Chancellor and only had an advisory role vis-à-vis the training of magistrates. Following the creation of the unified HM Courts Service (below) the training of magistrates also takes place under the JSB. As part of its general remit, the JSB provides a range of courses, materials and related support or advice to members of the judiciary at each stage of their careers. It has been to the fore in the development of various manuals - often in partnership with the Magistrates' Association and Justices' Clerks' Society – and notably was amongst the first bodies within the CJS to take the initiative on such issues as race, religion, discrimination, diversity, equality of treatment and human rights from the 1980s onwards. The JSB is based at Millbank Tower, Westminster. Post-creation of the MOJ, the JSB continues to be responsible for the

---

[9] Also coroners and members of ordinary tribunals.

[10] The Judicial Discipline Regulations (Prescribed Procedures) 2006 (SI 2006/676) contain details of other complaints which the OJC is or is not competent to consider.

[11] Similarly, those re tribunal judges or members are first referred to the tribunal president. The OJC deals with such complaints where there is no such president. Special arrangements exist re complaints against judicial office holders within tribunals.

[12] Statutory Instrument 247 of 2004. Similar rules apply to tribunals, coroners, etc.

training of the judiciary. Since April 2006, it has reported to the Lord Chief Justice within the management structure of the JO (above).

The Judicial Appointments Commission (JAC)

'Judicial appointment' is a description that is applied to the process whereby someone is made a judge or magistrate, sometimes described as being appointed to judicial office. The term can also be used as a noun to describe any such office. Historically, judicial appointment was a closed, secretive and uncertain process in which a good deal took place off the record and on the basis of unpublished criteria. Particularly with more senior appointments it was reliant on 'old boy networks' and other informal measures such as, e.g. private conversations with or 'soundings' taken from existing judges and senior lawyers. The Constitutional Reform Act 2005 created an independent and transparent Judicial Appointments Commission (JAC) that began work in 2006. With a view to taking matters further, the MOJ Green Paper, *The Governance of Britain*[13] notes that:

> In England and Wales, until recently all judicial appointments were made or recommended by the Lord Chancellor. Since the JAC began work in 2006 the Lord Chancellor has retained a residual role in appointments, either in accepting the JAC's selection or rejecting a name or asking for it to be reconsidered ... The Constitutional Reform Act 2005 established the JAC as an independent body to select judicial office holders ... The Government is willing to look at the future of its role in judicial appointments: to consider going further than the present arrangement, including conceivably a role for Parliament itself, after consultation with the judiciary, Parliament and the public, if it is felt that there is a need.[14]

HM COURTS SERVICE (HMCS)

The Crown has held the responsibility for the running of the courts for many hundreds of years, this now being just one aspect of the work of the MOJ in providing a courts system to facilitate the hearing of criminal cases and civil matters. This it does principally via HMCS, except that the administrative arrangements for the judicial functions of the House of Lords are administered directly by the Houses of Parliament. The various courts are noted under the heading *The Courts Structure: A Note*, below and broadly in ascending order of their jurisdiction and powers. It should be noted that both the rule of law and the requirement that a criminal suspect receive a fair trial envisage that there will be an adequate appeals process. Generally speaking, an accused person can appeal against conviction and/or sentence, e.g. following conviction in the magistrates

---

[13] Cm 7170.

[14] This will extend to the devolved administrations of Scotland and Northern Ireland.

court to the Crown Court, or if the conviction takes place in the Crown Court to the Court of Appeal (Criminal Division). There are other arrangements to deal with appeals on points of law (i.e. as opposed to the facts and merits of the case); and comparable arrangements exist in relation to civil and family matters. A prosecutor can appeal in certain circumstances, including on matters of law or, via the attorney general (*Chapter 5*), against unduly lenient sentences.

The Courts Service was launched in 1995 (without its modern pre-fix HM) as an executive agency of the then LCD. Its purpose was to handle the operational business of the Crown Court, county court and the existing Supreme Courts.[15] In 2001, the Auld Review[16] recommended the development of a single agency for the administration of justice, bringing together the then Magistrates' Courts Service and existing Courts Service into one unified administrative organization. The Courts Act 2003 contained the framework for HMCS which replaced the former Courts Service when the relevant provisions were implemented in 2005, at the same time linking the administration of magistrates' courts to its existing responsibilities. HMCS is an executive agency of the MOJ whose remit or mission is 'to deliver justice effectively and efficiently to the public'. At its web-site, HMCS sets out one of its main goals as follows:

> All citizens according to their differing needs are entitled to access to justice, whether as victims of crime, defendants accused of crimes, consumers in debt, children in need of care, or business people in commercial disputes. Our aim is to ensure that access is provided as quickly as possible and at the lowest cost consistent with open justice and that citizens have greater confidence in, and respect for, the system ....[17]

HMCS's strategic focus is thus on 'access to justice' (see, further, *Chapter 5*) as well as reducing cost, reducing delay and generating respect, which it claims will lead to a transformation of court services by 2010.

Geographically speaking, HMCS operates through 25 areas within seven regions of England and Wales, alongside a Royal Courts of Justice group whose role includes the administration of the Court of Appeal, High Court and Probate Service. It provides administration and support to all of these by way of a business strategy setting out the objectives for 'a modern, efficient service for the 21st century'. Aims set out in the HMCS business plan for the five years from 2007 are somewhat more wide-ranging, touching on general objectives of penal policy and crime reduction, and begin as follows:

---

[15] See the explanation under the heading *Supreme Court* later in the text.

[16] *A Review of the Criminal Courts of England and Wales* by The Rt. Hon. Lord Justice Auld (2001): see www.criminal-courts-review.org.uk

[17] www.hmcourts-service.gov.uk

To reduce crime and anti-social behaviour, protecting the rights of the law abiding citizen and making our communities safer. To protect the vulnerable, especially children at risk and the socially excluded. To enable people to resolve their problems better by promoting and delivering faster and more effective dispute resolution.

As with all other public services, HMCS works in partnership with other organizations, notably, outside of the MOJ, the Home Office, Office for Criminal Justice Reform, Crown Prosecution Service and the police. This work it does alongside a companion MOJ-led organization, the Tribunals Service (below). Thus, according to the Lord Falconer:

> In relation to the courts … changes are already starting to transform the delivery of services through creating a common focus on delivering a first class justice system for the public who use the courts. The challenge now is to deliver that vision in all courts across England and Wales consistently. A first step is the delivery of a small number of achievable commitments that will … bring about a step change in performance, a 'breakthrough' in the public's experience of the court system … Delivering this step change requires a partnership between all the parts of the system, led by HMCS staff, the judiciary and the magistracy … I have been visiting courts across the country listening, and talking to staff, judiciary, magistrates and delivery partners. Demonstrating the shared goal, all are working towards determining the best way to improve the public's experience of the justice system.[18]

Other responsibilities

Apart from administering courts of law, HMCS's multifarious responsibilities and activities cover such matters as:

- providing information about court locations;
- providing official forms;
- advertising staff vacancies and associated recruitment;
- wills and probate;
- arranging court hearings and court lists; and
- registering certain court outcomes or 'judgments' on various databases.

Court lists (i.e. the arrangements for hearings in relation to the Royal Courts of Justice, Crown Courts, selected county courts, as well as case archives and legal news, can be accessed through *Courtel* at its CourtServe web-site.[19] Magistrates' court lists are prepared at too short notice to be notified to such and updated effectively and accurately. Such information extends, e.g. to daily 'cause lists' as well as to those of the:

---

[18] At the MOJ web-site: www.justice.gov.uk
[19] www.courtserve2.net/court-lists

- Administrative Court and Divisional Courts of the High Court;
- Bankruptcy Court;
- Chancery Division;
- Commercial Court and Admiralty Court;
- Companies Court (including the Companies Court Winding Up List);
- Court of Appeal (Civil Division);
- Court of Appeal (Criminal Division);
- Family Division of the High Court;
- Patents County Court;
- Principal Registry of the Family Division (PRFD);
- Chancery Division of the High Court;
- Queen's Bench Division of the High Court (including the Queen's Bench Masters List);
- Supreme Court Costs Office;[20] and the
- Technology and Construction Court.

There is a separate Jury Central Summoning Bureau (JCSB).[21]

The courts structure: a note

The courts of England and Wales are broadly speaking divided as between criminal courts and civil courts although there are various overlapping jurisdictions where, e.g. a predominantly 'criminal court' will undertake civil functions and vice-versa.[22] Broadly in ascending order of jurisdiction and powers the criminal court structure comprises:

- magistrates' courts;
- youth courts (for people below the age of 18 years);
- the Crown Court;
- the High Court (mainly the Divisional Court of the Queens Bench Division (QBD));
- Court of Appeal (Criminal Division); and
- House of Lords (administered by the Houses of Parliament).

On the civil side the court structure comprises:

- the small claims court;
- county courts;

---

[20] See the explanation under the heading *Supreme Court* later in the text.
[21] See www.dca.gov.uk/consult/juries/summoning
[22] There are separate arrangements in Scotland and Northern Ireland.

- the family court (including magistrates' family proceedings courts);
- the High Court (including the Family Division and Chancery Division);
- the Court of Appeal (Civil Division); and
- the House of Lords (administered by the Houses of Parliament).

Whilst the House of Lords (and in future the new Supreme Court (below)) is the highest national court in the UK, ever since the implementation of the Human Rights Act 1998, the European Convention On Human Rights (ECHR) has been directly enforceable in national courts and with a right of appeal to the European Court of Human Rights. This and related matters are dealt with in *Chapter 6*. A brief outline of each of the UK national courts noted above appears within *Appendix III* to this work along with a note of the judges who sit in those courts.

Enforcement of court orders

Another key development that affects all courts, criminal and civil, should perhaps be noted and is represented in mechanisms for the fairer and more effective enforcement of court orders. This is noted in *Chapter 3* in relation to criminal matters. In relation to civil orders the Tribunals, Courts and Enforcement Act 2007 (TCE) now regulates the powers of bailiffs when executing warrants and other court orders. Speaking just before the TCE became law, Vera Baird QC, the then responsible MOJ minister, stated that:

> The Bill also powerfully strengthens the regulation of enforcement agents. In future, nobody will be able to act as a bailiff unless they are personally certificated to do so by a county court judge. They will each have to pass a training programme, deposit a bond, which can be forfeited for misconduct, and demonstrate to the judge that they are, in every way, fit and proper to do this important and sensitive job. There will be new court procedures to call to account abuses of power and misconduct and the fee structure will be reformed and simplified to discourage abuses aimed at making money out of debtors. Enforcement officers will be taught to manage vulnerable people in a proper way ... We are determined to get rid of the cowboy enforcement agents, who are unregulated and do not work to acceptable standards and to do that as soon as the [TCE] becomes law. In due course, we want to move licensing and regulation into the hands of the Security Industries Association (SIA) and we want to ensure that their longer-term regime will be equally tough. I have no doubt that local county courts will exercise their new responsibilities with great rigour ... There has been much talk of enabling enforcement agents to use reasonable force to gain entry into a home to collect a debt. That provision will not be enacted until the full SIA licensing system comes into force and even then it will only be available as an absolute last resort if a county court judge agrees to it after a detailed inquiry.

THE NEW SUPREME COURT

There was and is an 'old Supreme Court'. Broadly speaking the description applied to the High Court and Court of Appeal as an entity (see *Appendix III*). The UK's first Supreme Court in the new and full sense of that phrase was created by the Constitutional Reform Act 2005. Following a substantial lead-in time to allow for general planning and the location and conversion of accommodation it is now scheduled to open in October 2009.[23] Once in being, the court will take over the judicial role of the House of Lords – the work and jurisdiction of the present Appellate Committee of the House of Lords - so as to become the final court of appeal for England, Wales and Northern Ireland with regard to criminal cases and also with regard to civil matters (including in the latter instance in relation to Scotland). Centrally, it will hear appeals on arguable points of law where these are of general public importance.[24]

It is envisaged that the new Supreme Court will be run not by HMCS or the Houses of Parliament but by a new and dedicated agency currently being described as 'Supreme Court Staff' who, as with HMCS staff, will be civil servants. The President of the Supreme Court (initially a senior Law Lord) and its chief executive will have responsibility for its day-to-day administration, staffing and operation. In balancing independence with ministerial accountability for the expenditure of public money there will be limited links with the Lord Chancellor and MOJ, presumably of the kind envisaged by 'The Concordat' (see earlier section).

The court will also assume the jurisdiction of the Judicial Committee of the Privy Council (see generally under that heading below).

The present Law Lords will become the first justices of the Supreme Court that will have 12 members. Existing Law Lords will technically remain non-debating members of the House of Lords after the Supreme Court is created; but new judges appointed to the Supreme Court on or after its creation will be styled 'Justices of the Supreme Court' and will not be members of the House of Lords.

The Supreme Court can be seen as part of a sequence of events designed to separate further the Executive and Legislature from the Judiciary – whilst retaining lines of democratic accountability – that have arisen due to both domestic UK needs and European obligations. Indeed, the Government has indicated that the court 'will provide greater clarity in our constitutional arrangements by further separating the judiciary from the legislature'. It will be housed in Middlesex Guildhall off Parliament Square, Westminster (opposite the

---

[23] This is the latest of a series of dates that have been announced but would now seem to be reasonably firm in the light of construction and renovation work starting. The court has its own web-site at www.justice.gov.uk/whatwedo/supremecourt.htm

[24] The MOJ has UK-wide responsibilities whereas HMCS is limited to England and Wales.

Houses of Parliament and alongside Westminster Abbey and the Treasury). The Guildhall is being renovated for this purpose to a design that is 'both imaginative and respects the historic fabric and architectural merits of the building'.[25]

Consultation on rules for the Supreme Court is being carried out in accordance with the terms of the 2005 Act (and associated delegated legislation) [26] from 2007 under the senior Law Lord, Lord Bingham of Cornhill, who has sought views on the draft UK Supreme Court Rules.

THE PRIVY COUNCIL

The Privy Council (PC) is in general terms the Sovereign's private council of advisers as reconstituted in 1679 and nowadays consists of eminent people appointed by the sovereign and who are styled 'privy councillor' and entitled to be formally addressed as 'The Right Honourable'. In that context, the PC is presided over by the Sovereign or his or her representative. For justice purposes, the Judicial Committee of the Privy Council connotes something different, viz the Law Lords wearing 'a different hat' and sitting as a committee to hear appeals from certain Commonwealth or former Commonwealth countries. They are sometimes helped in this regard by expert foreign judges.

The jurisdiction of the PC extends over dominion territories, or former such territories that have opted to continue with this last avenue of appeal - as an adjunct to their own national arrangements and appeal framework. Unlike

---

[25] Middlesex Guildhall is a Grade II listed building re which the former DCA commissioned refurbishment plans. Developments were initially delayed by choice of a suitable building and there have been mixed comments about whether the interior of the building should be interfered with to create courtrooms, etc; or indeed whether The Guildhall can provide suitable accommodation. However, various commentators have pointed to the unsuitability of the existing facilities within the House of Lords where committee rooms rather than courtrooms are regularly used for court proceedings. In June 2007, the MOJ declared that 'The highest court in the land should be open, accessible and independent. The Middlesex Guildhall will be transformed into a building suitable for such an important institution and enable the court to take its rightful place alongside its prestigious neighbours on Parliament Square. [We believe that] we have struck the right balance of preserving a historic building while bringing new life to that building and providing for greater public access'. After a rigorous public procurement exercise, Kier Group were appointed to carry out the renovation at an estimated cost of £56.9m in 'set up-costs' (£36.7m of renovation costs which will be paid for by an annual lease charge of £2.1m over 30 years as per the original estimates). The additional £20.2m was to cover professional adviser fees, programme team costs, furniture, IT services and library costs. (MOJ Press Release). The plans can be viewed at www.feildenandmawson.com

[26] See Statutory Instrument 227 of 2006.

rulings of the House of Lords, those of the PC are persuasive rather than binding under the doctrine of precedent.

ADMINISTRATIVE JUSTICE AND TRIBUNALS

Developments comparable to those already described in relation to HMCS are underway at the MOJ in relation to the Tribunals Service (TS); except that the TS, unlike HMCS, operates UK-wide. Before being brought together by the former DCA in 2006, various kinds of tribunals fell within the remit of a range of government departments. A now unified TS administers tribunals at all levels and covering a wide range of potential disputes in relation to matters of administrative justice, in broad terms; hearing appeals against decision-making by officials rather than by judges and magistrates – but that are nonetheless subject to rules of fair treatment, relevance, reasonableness, consistency and transparency. A wide range of tribunals exist to review decision-making by government departments or other state sponsored agencies and a considerable body of law - known as administrative law - has developed over the last 50 years in particular. In certain instances, members of the judiciary sit as 'judicial' or 'legal' members of a tribunal, often as a qualified chair.

The Tribunals Service (TS)

At its web-site,[27] the MOJ states that it aims 'to improve the way in which disputes over administrative decisions affecting individuals ... are dealt with'. An overall MOJ strategy is 'to reduce the need for people to go to a tribunal' by developing various forms of conflict resolution and dispute resolution (sometimes described as 'alternative dispute resolution' (ADR)). Where this cannot be achieved, tribunals hear cases of many kinds, including those relating to asylum, revenue matters, immigration and asylum,[28] agricultural lands, open competition, social security benefits, employment, gender recognition, charities, war pensions, mental impairment and discrimination. The TS processes these cases and provides information and support to the various people who are involved in tribunal cases, including applicants, appellants, witnesses and various legal and other professional practitioners.

The Council on Administrative Justice and Tribunals (CAJT)

The CAJT replaced the former Council on Tribunals under the Tribunals Courts and Enforcement Act 2007 (TCE) that contains a wide range of provisions for reform of the tribunal system and changed eligibility requirements for judicial

---

[27] www.justice.gov.uk
[28] For UK border controls, see the companion to this work, *The New Home Office*.

office (as well as measures covering the regulation of bailiffs and enforcement by seizure and sale of goods; increased effectiveness for the enforcement of civil court judgements; and measures to protect the over-indebted). Around 80 tribunals fall under the oversight of the council, and it must be consulted on the procedural rules for all tribunals. Within broader MOJ policies, it seeks to ensure, among other things, that tribunals and inquiries:

- are accessible to all;
- are quick, informal, and as cheap as possible;
- provide the right to an oral hearing in public;
- give reasons for their decisions; and
- are seen to be independent, impartial and fair to all.

As with its forerunner, a focus of CAJT is likely to be on common performance standards, fair, open and straightforward procedures, adequate training for tribunal members and administrators, efficient, user-friendly administration and promoting and sharing best practice. The council must publish a statutory annual report to the Lord Chancellor and relevant Scottish ministers, and various special reports and guidance on key, tribunal-related matters. In the final run up to the TCE, the then relevant MOJ minister, Vera Baird QC, stated that the Act would speed up justice and make processes easier for the public to understand:

> I am pleased the TCE Bill is nearing completion. Bringing most tribunals together and harmonising their procedures will help people to find their way around the system and get solutions to their issues more quickly and efficiently. We will set up a network of appeal hearing centres in major centres to promote ready access to more justice services.

Complaints about tribunal members

As already indicated, there is a comparable system to that for judges and magistrates for people wishing to complain about a tribunal judge or member. Potential complainants should normally contact the relevant tribunal office to establish whether that complaint should be sent to the regional chair, the tribunal president or, if there is no chair or president, to the OJC (above).

COMMUNITY JUSTICE

Community justice emerged as a government initiative as part of the programme for civil renewal and active citizenship which David Blunkett MP initiated in 2003 during his time as home secretary. Modelled on a scheme at Red Hook in New York, a community justice centre was established in Liverpool and similar arrangements have been set up in Salford and other places. Responsibility was placed with the DCA at an early stage. The MOJ asserts that:

> Community justice meets the needs of people living in the local area, encouraging them to take ownership of their police, court, types of crime tackled and unpaid work. Community justice can also be a resource for non-court based activities such as counselling and advice services, mentoring, youth clubs, volunteering opportunities and much more.[29]

Its main features (summarised) are that:

- the courts and local judiciary are connected to the community;
- justice is seen to be done;
- cases are handled robustly and speedily;
- a strong independent district judge or bench of magistrates leads a problem solving approach;
- problem solving and finding solutions help offenders to break the cycle of offending;
- a team of agencies works together to deliver an end-to-end service to offenders, victims and the local community;
- the community has a say in the unpaid work to be done by offenders, so repairing harm and raising confidence; and
- offenders are reintegrated into their communities.

A statutory power intended specifically for community justice centres enables a court to review each offender's progress as he or she carries out community orders, and if necessary the court can modify the requirements or conditions that are part and parcel of a generic community sentence (see, generally, *Chapter 7*).

The Government states that community justice is an integral part of its Respect Agenda, but its scope extends far beyond anti-social behaviour (ASB).

---

[29] More information appears at www.communityjustice.gov.uk

CHAPTER 3

Prisons, Probation and Parole

CHAPTER 3

Prisons, Probation and Parole

As noted in *Chapter 1*, a central feature of the Home Office split was the transfer out from the Home Office to the Ministry of Justice (MOJ) of a range of responsibilities in relation to prisons, probation, parole and allied services. The MOJ, which already by that time listed crime reduction amongst its key objectives, thus acquired new means towards achieving that end. According the MOJ at its web-site:[1]

> We will reduce re-offending and protect the public. This Government has changed the face of penal policy over the last ten years. We have recognised the need to intervene as early as possible to prevent children who might drift into crime from doing so. We have developed interventions in the Youth Justice System that aim to reduce the chances of re-offending. We have unequivocally and unashamedly focused policy on ensuring that the dangerous offender remains in prison until he or she ceases to be a danger. We have given the law enforcement authorities the tools to bear down on anti-social behaviour. We have increased the range of punishments available. And we have recognised the need to do all we can to reduce re-offending – by massively increasing drug treatments and offending behaviour interventions; more work with offenders in prison and on release, tougher community penalties, more unpaid work, more restorative justice and greater monitoring and support for those who have offended when they are in the community ...

The MOJ describes this as 'a shift in policy which ... is beginning to show results', with proven re-offending rates falling by some two per cent between 2000 and 2004 for both adult and young offenders, as well as an increase in the number of dangerous offenders being 'off the streets'. Overall, the MOJ points to a reduction in crime.[2] But as the MOJ also notes: 'We know that 50 per cent of the resources to reduce re-offending lie outside the MOJ. This means we must jointly commission and work in partnership to deliver'.

Reducing re-offending
The MOJ acknowledges that offenders are amongst the most excluded groups within society and that reducing re-offending means further developing partnership work and building alliances at regional and local level. It sees this

---

[1] www.justice.gov.uk

[2] Something that would appear to be at odds with the increased use of imprisonment described later in this chapter, or a consequence of it, according to points of view.

challenge as transforming offenders into citizens together with appropriate monitoring and supervision, with departments and agencies working together to tackle drug and alcohol abuse, improving basic skills, tackling offending behaviour and improving the chances of released offenders getting work:

> It means helping [offenders] to get decent accommodation and ... working with the children and families of offenders and trying to break the cycle of offending that can afflict families between generations ... This is why we are driving ahead with an ambitious programme of reform that includes developing a new system which will enable us to commission services from a range of providers and work in partnership with a range of agencies. It means introducing a named offender manager for every offender and a focus on local delivery. In consultation with the courts, and working in partnership with the police and the Third Sector,[3] we will commission provision to allow intensive community sentences to be given that are tough, safe and effective. They include specified high minimum contact times and daily reporting backed by a curfew and electronic monitoring at night ... It is important for public protection that we address the group that are sentenced to less than 12 months in custody. We know that over 70 per cent of these offenders re-offend, often soon after release; short sentences might mean that some offenders become more, not less, likely to re-offend. We must ensure they get to the most effective sentence available, which in many cases will be a tough community sentence.

Hence the MOJ promises that it will among other things:

- continue to improve the design and delivery of the more than 24,000 offending behaviour programmes and 12,000 drug treatments every year across prison and probation services to drive down re-offending;
- work right across government to improve accommodation, education and employment outcomes on release;
- develop new ways, through commissioning and offender management, of focusing resources on the most prolific offenders and delivering more effectively elsewhere (specifically developing a demonstration project to commission provision that better allows intensive community orders, those containing quite substantial requirements, to be provided);
- provide more information to sentencers on the effectiveness of interventions (see, generally, *Chapter 7*);
- ensure that the widest range of Third Sector organizations are involved in correctional services planning and delivery, and reduce obstacles to this.

---

[3] Meaning charities, voluntary organizations and forms of social enterprise. See, also, the wealth of information available at www.thirdsector.co.uk

The MOJ also recognises that protecting the public is not just about criminal justice. It notes that the Family Justice System (FJS) has a significant role to play in child protection; in protecting victims of domestic violence; and that children involved in public law care cases are often in an extremely vulnerable position.

> We want to achieve better and improved outcomes for the child by ensuring that all agencies work together collaboratively to establish, safe, permanent and timely results for the children involved in these cases.

It notes that domestic violence accounts for 17 per cent of reported crime – one incident being reported to the police every minute. The FJS also plays an important role in protecting victims of domestic violence – so that between 2003 and 2005 an average of over 24,000 civil injunctions a year were made under the Family Law Act 1996 – as does the Prevention from Harassment Act 1997 in both the civil courts and the criminal courts. The MOJ has an important role in tackling violence against women and asserts that it will continue to ensure the best possible service to victims of domestic violence, through specialist domestic violence courts and Independent Domestic Violence Advisers.

Protecting the public is an objective that the MOJ shares with a range of other government departments and services, including the Home Office, Office of the Attorney General and the new Department of Children, Families and Schools, including via various Cabinet Office committees.[4]

PRISON

By mid-2007 the prison population of England and Wales had reached an all time high of 81,016. This compared with 61,467 when the New Labour Government came to power in 1997 and just over 45,000 in the mid-1980s. The increase means that the UK now imprisons around 150 people per 100,000 of the population, the highest proportion in Europe or most other western-style democracies – apart, notably, from the USA.[5] At that time, amidst Government plans to build 9,500 more prison places by 2012 at a capital cost of over £1.5 billion, some 500 prisoners per day were being held, at least for a time, in police station cells or, at one stage, ill-equipped 'day cells' at courthouses under Operation Safeguard. 'Quick build' temporary accommodation, redundant army barracks and ships

---

[4] This united front is further dealt with in the companion volume, *The New Home Office*.

[5] The USA rate is around 350 people per 100,000 but there are significant variations between states. The UK prison population peaked at around 81,400. A great deal of information about prison populations, the potentially negative effects of overcrowding and the seemingly inconsistent or disproportionate use of imprisonment in the UK is available from the Prison Reform Trust: www.prisonreform.org

were all on stand-by in case matters got worse. By the time that the Ministry of Justice (MOJ) was announced[6] a general scheme for the early release of non-dangerous short-term offenders was already underway and a new Management of Offenders and Sentencing Bill was before Parliament.[7] According to the *Guardian* newspaper concerning the growing use of court cells:

> A special agreement has already been reached with the Courts Service for six centres to be used … the [MOJ] is trying to negotiate for two more Crown Court centres for prisoners who are now, in effect, queuing to get into jail.[8]

In response, Paul Cavadino, chief executive of the crime reduction charity, the National Association for the Rehabilitation of Offenders (Nacro) wrote in reply:

> Police cells have no facilities for detoxification, counselling or support for vulnerable prisoners. One-third of all prison suicides occur in the first week of custody, and deaths of prisoners have risen alarmingly … as detention in police cells has increasingly become the norm for newly received inmates … Court cells are even less suitable than police cells — they are not designed to hold prisoners overnight, they are simply intended for prisoners to sit in during the day while they wait to go to into court. A typical cell has no natural light and is little more than half the size of a Victorian-built prison cell; when a mattress is placed on the floor, the end curls up against the wall … Any solution must involve tackling sentencing head on.[9]

It was in this context that the MOJ was launched. Initially, the former Home Office and now MOJ early-release scheme envisaged that between 1,200 and 1,800 short–term and non-dangerous prisoners would be released 18 days early, Lord Falconer, the then Lord Chancellor, subsequently indicating as such release began that in a full year about 25,000 prisoners would become eligible for this variety of early release. It was the first general use of such powers in modern times and seemingly had been resisted until the point at which it became clear that the Operation Safeguard (above) was unsustainable.

Some reasons for the increase

Commentators debate the exact causes for the gradual rise in the use of imprisonment, which in more recent times would appear to be driven by a range of factors, some of a concrete kind, others attitudinal, including (but not

---

6 May 2007: see, generally, *Chapter 1.*
7 The 2007 Bill contains proposals designed to reduce re-offending through improved offender management and it would allow the MOJ or NOMS to commission services from the public or private with a view to raising standards and supporting innovation.
8 20 June 2007.
9 *The Guardian,* 21 June 2007.

necessarily focused entirely on) the kind of offenders who have filled up the prisons. These factors include (in no particular hierarchy of significance):

- politicians 'talking tough' about law and order issues alongside the introduction of more dynamic and pro-active forms of policing as described in the companion to this work, *The New Home Office*;
- the introduction of various mandatory or minimum sentences, especially indefinite sentences for public protection from dangerous and/or sexual offenders known as imprisonment for public protection (IPP);[10]
- a tightening-up of enforcement strategies with regard to community sentences, parole and other forms of release from prison accompanied by more automatic types of breach procedure or recall to prison (see also later in this chapter under *Parole*);
- some reduction in the level of discretion allowed to courts, probation officers, or in some cases the police, to take a more lenient view;
- a considerable increase in the number of new offences since 1997 and the creation of the anti-social behaviour order that can have the effect of criminalising low-level or nuisance type behaviour at the breach stage;[11]
- the 'foreign prisoner crisis' wherein it was discovered that prisoners were not being deported at the end of their sentences in accordance with court recommendations, leading to many of them simply being set free (or, in some instances, held for long periods whilst their case was processed);[12]
- non-implementation of key provisions of the Criminal Justice Act 2003 concerning a new sentence of 'custody plus' under which sentences under 12 months were to be served partially in prison, but largely in the community (the 'plus' element);[13]
- an associated failure to resource community sentences to a level that would allow these to be effectively used in place of custody;
- an apparent refusal by sentencing courts to heed exhortations (though some would say attempts at 'judicial interference') by some politicians, reformers and other liberally-minded groups to use custody more sparingly; although sentencers might also point out that they were often being urged to be tougher and criticised if offenders were seen as 'walking away' from court or re-offended;
- the continued use of prisons for:[14]

---

[10] Or sometimes 'sentences for public protection' (SPP).
[11] For further explanation, see *Chapter 4* of *The New Home Office*.
[12] And led to the resignation of the home secretary, Charles Clarke in 2006.
[13] See, also, the comments in *Chapter 7*.
[14] It is impossible to rehearse here all the arguments concerning individual groups, some of which can be found in the source materials noted at the end of this book. The MOJ

- many minor offenders who arguably need not be there;
- women who may have been treated disproportionately compared with men committing similar offences;
- young people against whom much law enforcement is targeted ;
- people from black and ethnic minority groups;
- people from other vulnerable groups including those who are mentally impaired and who maybe ought to be in a suitable hospital;
- a general hardening of attitudes post-the World Trade Center attack of 11 September 2001 and the London bombings of 7 July 2005;
- threats from organized crime, including its now global aspects; and
- a rise in cyber-crime, a term that has come to be used to describe a wide range of internet-based offences from fraud to paedophilia.

Despite an increasing prison population, the sanction of imprisonment has for a long time been regarded as something to be reserved for the most serious and dangerous offenders and viewed as a sentence of last resort; this being reinforced by both a statutory sentencing framework (*Chapter 7*) and case law.

HM Prison Service: A note

Her Majesty's Prison Service (HMPS) has been an executive agency since 1993 and part of the National Offender Management Service (NOMS) since 2003. It is led by a director general who is responsible for the delivery of services and what are sometimes described as 'operational matters' – a distinction that has not always been a straightforward one in practice. The Prisons Board is HMPS's senior management team chaired by the director general with executive directors covering such areas as health care, offending behaviour programmes, custody and finance. There are also non-executive directors from outside of HMPS. The service employs around 40,000 staff, nearly two-thirds of whom are uniformed prison officers while over 1,000 are members of the 'governor grades'. Prison officers with basic internal nursing training are employed as hospital officers in male prisons. Qualified nurses are employed in women's establishments and some are employed in male prisons.

HMPS operates primarily under the Prisons Act 1952, Prison Rules 1999 and an accumulation of internal Prison Service Orders (PSOs), Prison Service Instructions (PSIs) and Prison Service Manuals which in combination deal with every aspect of prison life (with comparable provisions for young offenders). Over the years its former relative isolation has been gradually replaced by way of working partnerships with other agencies, particularly with the National

has certain key duties and responsibilities concerning fairness and equality treatment and the promulgation of related information as noted in *Chapter 6*.

Probation Service (NPS) and both the voluntary sector and private sector organizations. All prison establishments – including those managed by the private sector – are styled 'Her Majesty's' (or HM) Prison (e.g. HM Prison Wormwood Scrubs). The management of a number of prisons is contracted out to the private sector and some new prisons are currently being planned or are under construction, mostly designed, built, managed and financed by the private sector. Such prisons have a director rather than a governor and are linked to the MOJ via one of its own controllers. Each prison is inspected periodically by HM Inspector of Prisons and has an Independent Monitoring Board (IMB). There is also a Prisons and Probation Ombudsman (for further detail, see *Chapter 4*).

Prison governors and prison officers

All or any members of what are generally termed the 'governor grades' may be described as a 'governor', i.e. an HMPS employee who holds that grade even though he or she is not necessarily a 'governing Governor' in charge of an individual prison establishment or working, usually leading a unit, at HMPS headquarters in London. Governors form a separate hierarchy above the various ranks of prison officer. Other key prison staff include prison probation officers who work inside a prison linking it to the community and medical officers; prison doctors who advise governors on health matters and prepare reports for courts on prisoners, as well as providing healthcare for them. Education officers, usually qualified teachers, run full-time or part time education courses, including evening classes (all according to available resources and funding); and chaplains and other spiritual leaders provide opportunities for worship, counselling and pastoral care, supported by visiting ministers of denominations and faiths with fewer adherents. There is a Prison Governors' Association (PGA).

Prison officers are the frontline uniformed officers in every HMPS prison (they may be known as 'guards' in a private prison). There are various ranks, including senior officer and principal officer; and it is now possible to progress from officer to governor. Many belong to the Prison Officers Association (POA).[15]

PROBATION

In the context of this chapter, probation is a convenient way in which to refer to all forms of community sentence, community sentences now being general in nature and involving a menu of possible requirements that courts can select from in order to construct what is known as a generic community sentence. This will be geared both to the offence or offences in question and the particular offender. Requirements range from supervision through unpaid work to a curfew and

---

[15] In a privately managed prison the terminology is different: see on this page.

conditions of residence. There is also an emphasis on the treatment of drug and alcohol dependence. Electronic monitoring that can be added to such orders (and in some cases normally must be added). Similar requirements are used where someone is released early from prison, to cover their time in the community but when they are still, technically, serving a prison sentence.

The administration of community sentences is the province of the National Probation Service (NPS) arm of the National Offender Management Service (NOMS).[16] The use on the one hand of imprisonment and on the other of community sentences as per this section is directly inter-related and the idea that the arrangements for both should operate under one umbrella has much to commend it. Hence the creation of the first (then) Home Office director of correctional services,[17] Martin Narey, in 2003, and of NOMS itself as a fundamental reconstruction of the administrative arrangements within which HMPS (above) and the NPS operate, following proposals contained in *Managing Offenders, Reducing Crime*.[18] The HMPS/NPS/NOMS inter-relationship is also critical if sound plans are to be in place for the administration of sentences across the board – as part of what is sometimes called a 'seamless sentence', especially where, as part of this, supervision in the community follows imprisonment.

So too, it can be argued, should courts and sentencers be more closely involved than in the past in understanding and possibly influencing this overall process by developing closer links to NOMS. Arguments about the essential and constitutional need for courts, judges and magistrates to have their independence protected (*Chapter 2*)[19] are of a different order to those about whether, in terms of the best overall use of penal resources, they should have enhanced links with each other in this regard. According to the MOJ:

> At the heart of our vision is end-to-end case management for offenders, and a strong focus on commissioning the most effective interventions for men and women which will best support the management and rehabilitation of offenders. This includes the systematic identification of which interventions work best, encouraging providers to innovate to improve the effectiveness of interventions, making use of the fullest range of providers – including public, private and voluntary sectors – and the strategic management of providers with a strong focus on delivering outcomes.

---

[16] And so long as NOMS, HMPS and the NPS subsist in the way they did pre-MOJ.

[17] 'Corrections' is a term widely used to describe penal sanctions.

[18] Also known as 'the Carter Report'. Carter, P (2003), *Managing Offenders, Reducing Crime*, Prime Minister's Strategy Unit.

[19] The way in which judicial independence is protected is explained in *Chapter 2*.

The National Probation Service (NPS)

Until the late-1990s the Probation Service (as it was then called) was organized on a purely local basis under local Probation Committees later called Probation Boards, but with links to the Home Office with which it had a hesitant relationship. The NPS was created in 2001 and as already noted above, later became part of NOMS alongside HMPS; but an entirely separate entity under its own director. The NPS works closely with other criminal justice agencies, including the police service. For the most dangerous offenders, including sexual and violent offenders, the NPS is required by law to work in partnership to protect the public; so that, e.g. supervision plans are designed to minimise the risk to the public from violent or sexual offenders. Much of the work occurs under the umbrella of statutory Multi-agency Public Protection Arrangements (MAPPAs).

Probation officers

There are approximately 21,000 probation officers and other probation staff working across England and Wales. Many probation officers are seconded to youth offending teams (YOTS) responsible for offenders under the age of 18. Probation officers are highly trained professionals; they are to be distinguished from probation service officers (PSOs) who have more modest qualifications. Among other things, probation officers:

- prepare (mostly) written pre-sentence reports (PSRs) for courts and advise generally on the suitability for certain offenders of community sentences;
- supervise offenders in the community where they are subject to what is now the generic community sentence (above);
- work in or in liaison with prisons to assist with sentence planning and liaise with the NPS in the area into which a prisoner will be released on parole or licence (below), as to which they may also be involved in preparing reports for the Parole Board or prison governor;
- work alongside drug workers, psychologists, psychiatrists, doctors and other professionals and practitioners to facilitate the use of such expertise;
- take part in (MAPPAs) (above);
- enforce court orders and parole or other release licences; and
- work with the victims of crime in certain circumstances; and prepare victim impact statements for courts at the time of sentencing.

Probation officers deal with some 200,000 cases at any one time, assisting courts with 246,000 PSRs (above) and 20,000 bail information reports per year, as well as supervision extending to over eight million hours of unpaid work by offenders. Before forming certain opinions about the appropriateness or otherwise of custody or a community sentence, a court must 'take into account all such information as is available to it about the circumstances of the offence or (as the case may be) of the offence or offences associated with it, including any aggravating factors or mitigating factors' (section 156(1) Criminal Justice Act 2003). This applies to decisions about:

- the 'serious enough' community sentence threshold and the extent of restriction of liberty created by a generic community sentence; and
- the 'so serious' custody threshold.

At its discretion, a court is able to take 'any available information' into account when deciding upon the suitability of a community sentence for a given offender.[20] At this stage, the contents of a PSR play a critical role.

Probation officers, seconded to the prison, who work alongside prison officers, undertake rehabilitation and pre-release work, liaise with prisoners' home probation officers, write reports for discretionary release purposes and advise HMPS management on issues affecting throughcare or sentence planning.

Background

Probation work developed from the early part of the 20th century to regulate good behaviour and provide contact with a befriending probation officer. The service was then primarily a welfare-based agency that emerged from the early work of the London Police Court Mission and that of philanthropists such as Frederick Rainer. As time progressed, the make-up, content and context for what became probation orders made by courts developed and the work of probation officers gradually moved further and further away from its welfare roots – one original purpose of probation having been 'to advise, assist and befriend' the offender - to the extent that the NPS is nowadays sometimes described in terms of its enforcement/corrections role. In its modern form, according to the MOJ:

> Probation is about supervising convicted offenders in the community, [those people] subject to a court order and those released on licence from prison. Our priorities are to reduce re-offending and protect the public.

Hostels and other accommodation

A further core task of the NPS has been arranging accommodation for certain ex-prisoners and providing bail hostels or half-way houses for a range of people involved with the criminal courts; one purpose being to protect the public from offenders who pose a significant risk of harm to other people but who can be managed in the community. Enhanced forms of supervision for such offenders in

---

[20] But any failure to consider relevant matters might be in breach of human rights law.

accredited premises can nowadays typically includes security measures such as CCTV and alarm systems, a standard curfew from 11pm to 6am and a core regime which addresses offending behaviour.

PAROLE

The MOJ also oversees former Home Office responsibilities with regard to parole and the Parole Board. At its web-site, the MOJ describes its arm's length responsibility as follows:

> Some offenders are released from prison before their custodial sentence is due to end. Although the offender is released, they are still serving their sentence with conditions on their liberty. Many are released on licence - only the most serious and dangerous offenders go through the Parole Board process. The Parole Board is an independent body, which [is sponsored by the MOJ], that works with its criminal justice partners to protect the public by risk assessing prisoners to decide whether they can be safely released into the community.

This then is a high-risk area for decision making, where accountability and one poisoned chalice[21] have been passed from the home secretary to the Lord Chancellor. Logically, with prisons under the MOJ umbrella, the functions of the Parole Board are an extension of this. The parole process has become increasingly visible in modern times due to concerns about the release of prisoners who have gone on to re-offend in terms of a very serious offences, or have disappeared whilst on licence; or where a recommendation by a judge for deportation at the end of a foreign prisoner's sentence has not been pursued. This was when these functions still lay with the home secretary and they were a significant factor in Dr John Reid's conclusion that the 'old' Home Office was 'not fit for purpose'.

Parole and parole licences
Parole is a generic term used to describe the 'back end' processes of criminal justice via which decisions concerning the early release of individual prisoners are made at the discretion of the (now) Lord Chancellor, i.e. whereby prisoners are placed on parole and made subject to a parole licence containing various

---

[21] Both Dr Reid and his predecessor Charles Clarke were castigated by the media. The latter's resignation came in the wake of the 'foreign prisoner crisis'. In other cases, offenders who had been risk-assessed and released on parole went on commit further serious offences, including murder and rape. Government responses included an all round tightening-up of the parole process and a requirement that all Parole Board decisions in favour of release be unanimous. See, further, the companion volume to this work, *The New Home Office*.

requirements and stipulations. Parole eligibility depends on the type of sentence, involved, its length and any tariff set by the judge.

Parole is granted by the Lord Chancellor following a recommendation by the Parole Board. It can also be granted directly by the Lord Chancellor: it is an *executive* rather than a *judicial* decision; but it involves a duty of fairness that is nowadays underpinned by considerations of human rights.

The Parole Board

In particular, the final recommendation of the Parole Board will rest on risk assessments and reports by HMPS staff, including in many instances psychiatrists or psychologists, and any NPS staff who have been closely involved. The Parole Board is an independent, non-executive, non-departmental public body (NDPB) that as already intimated makes risk-assessments to inform decisions by the Lord Chancellor concerning the release or recall to prison of those prisoners affected by the provisions. Parole guidelines and statutory directions issued by the Lord Chancellor set out the criteria to be applied and procedures to be followed. The board consists of a chair and over 80 members including active or otherwise retired judges, psychiatrists, chief probation officers and criminologists — as well as members with no direct experience of the Criminal Justice System (CJS). Decisions are made 'on the papers' but the prisoner may be interviewed by a member of the parole panel (below) or granted an oral hearing before the panel. The board publishes an annual report.

Individual decisions are arrived at by a panel made up of members the Parole Board convened to assess an individual application (in practice panels may deal with several such applications or aspects of them at one sitting). The board meets in panels of (normally) three or four members. Decisions take account of the prisoner's responses to his or her imprisonment, including, e.g. the courses that he or she has undertaken whilst in prison and the education and offending behaviour programmes that he or she has participated in. Similarly, the prisoner's wider history, background and performance in and out of prison fall to be considered. Decisions also take into account any comments made by the judge who passed sentence. In some instances there is direct consultation with that judge and/or the Lord Chief Justice. Victims also now have a voice through a Public Protection Advocacy Scheme (*Chapter 8*).

Ombudsmen, Inspectors and Monitors

CHAPTER 4

Ombudsmen, Inspectors and Monitors

Within any large scale public undertaking – and especially given modern-day operating methods, targets, objectives and funding – there is a need for some kind of external scrutiny or audit. Any lingering sense that justice-related functions might be immune from such processes is long gone. Each of the services that make up the justice system has its own appropriate inspection arrangements and sometimes other checks and balances exist. In accordance with the principles of judicial independence noted in *Chapters 2* and *6*, judges, magistrates and tribunal members are not themselves inspected in relation to their judicial functions, but their underlying administrations are, for their general efficiency, effectiveness and delivery. Even this can come close to judicial scrutiny if matters such as waiting times for cases to be dealt with, delays and throughput are brought into the balance sheet. Hence there are various safeguards within the work and remit of relevant inspectorates. There is now, at least, an independent Office for Judicial Complaints (OJC) albeit not one that is concerned with the merits of individual court or tribunal decisions. Those merits are challenged via appeals in the courts (*Chapter 2* and *Appendix III*).

Concern has tended to move away from a need to insulate the judiciary from inspectors[1] towards fear of cross-justice inspectorates. If warning be needed in this regard it was sounded by the House of Lords early in 2007 when rebel peers led by the former inspector of prisons, Lord David Ramsbotham, defeated Government moves to create a combined Criminal Justice Inspectorate.[2] Beyond inspectorates, this chapter also looks briefly at the role of the Prisons and Probation Ombudsman and Independent Monitoring Boards (IMBs) (formerly Boards of Visitors to prisons). These are not inspection roles but both represent an external eye on an otherwise largely closed world – and both now belong within the MOJ 'family'. This chapter also notes various other external roles.

---

[1] But similar concerns may continue to exist within other justice services with regard to aspects of professional integrity as opposed to general missions or aims.

[2] Not, perhaps, the kind of move that would have been made by any Government steeped in constitutional awareness: *Chapter 6*. It had been claimed that this would rationalise the use of resources, avoid duplication, allow data to be shared and problems attributable to inter-agency, or multi-agency, aspects of work to be better tackled. Critics focused on the concentration of power, information and influence that would fall into the hands of a single inspector who might be uncomfortably close to Government and vulnerable to control, manipulation, etc.

INSPECTORATES

Various inspectorates exist across the justice system – independently of the MOJ or the head of the agency concerned, usually led by a 'chief inspector' – whose role and responsibility it is to examine the work and performance etc. of a given agency and to report directly to Parliament. The paragraphs below cover some of the main inspectorates.

HM Inspectorate of Court Administration (HMICA)

HMICA is a statutory independent body headed by a chief inspector and with direct accountability to the Lord Chancellor. After taking over the former and separate Magistrates' Court Service Inspectorate, HMICA is now responsible for the inspection of the organization of the Crown Court, county courts and magistrates' courts, Children and Family Court Advisory Support Services (CAFCASS) functions in England and Wales and joint inspections of Criminal Justice Systems[3] and Joint Area Reviews with other inspectorates of children's services. It also inspects the Northern Ireland Court Service by invitation.

HMICA inspects and reports to the Lord Chancellor on the services provided by the magistrates' courts, Crown Court and county court. The Chief Inspector provides the Lord Chancellor with independent assurance on the operation of court administration as part of an overall 'assurance' concerning the operation and performance management regimes of HM Courts Service (*Chapter 2*).

HM Inspectorate of Prisons

This office was originally exercised within the internal structure of HMPS and the post-holder was a member of the then Prisons Board, to which the inspector also reported in confidence. Following the May Report (1979) an independent office was created, with the chief inspector reporting to the home secretary. The Criminal Justice Act 1982 placed the inspectorate on a statutory footing and created the title HM Chief Inspector of Prisons.

Since the time of one of the first independent inspectors of prisons, His Honour Sir Stephen Tumim, the role has enjoyed a relatively high public profile with successive chief inspectors interpreting their role as including the raising of public awareness about prison conditions, extending on occasion to issues of a campaigning nature. As a result, their relationship with ministers and HMPS has not always been easy – which might be thought to be a good thing if the role is to be properly carried out. Both Stephen Tumim and his successor, General Sir David Ramsbotham challenged existing prison regimes; the latter coming into

---

[3] It is interesting that the MOJ identifies these in the plural: also that a joint inspection function continues notwithstanding the failure to establish an MOJ-wide inspectorate.

direct confrontation with the home secretary (to whom he reported at that time), Michael Howard MP, concerning, among other things, the extent and purpose of the inspection role. Anne Owers, formerly director of the legal and human rights-based organization, JUSTICE, was appointed to the post in 2001 and many of her reports have proved equally searching and critical.

Each prison is inspected periodically by the inspector or his or her team of full-time or specialist inspectors (the latter may be attached to the inspection team for a given purpose). The inspectorate publishes an annual report and a report of each inspection, and also carries out thematic inspections on selected aspects of the prison system. Inspections have, e.g. included looking at the treatment of prisoners, regime quality, the morale of prisoners and staff, the quality of healthcare, the way a prison establishment is managed and the physical state of prison premises. HMPS must make and publish a considered reply. Concern has sometimes been expressed where the publication of reports or responses has been delayed within HMPS or, in the past, the Home Office.

HM Inspectorate of Probation

Before its links to the MOJ, the probation inspectorate had a long and respected history in the days of a purely local probation service structure before being formalised as a compact, autonomous unit, directly responsible to the home secretary and charged with inspecting the work of the National Probation Service (NPS). It also provided ministers and officials with advice on probation-related matters and sought to promote effective management and good practice. Chief inspectors have included outside people such as Professor Rod Morgan of Bristol University (later, and for a time, the chair of the Youth Justice Board (YJB)) but most day-to-day inspection staff have been drawn from within the (mainly higher) ranks of the NPS and with direct experience in the probation field, often having worked up through the grades. Suitably qualified people from other professions have also been attached to inspection teams.

Generally speaking, there have been two types of inspection: area inspections, when two or three aspects of work (e.g. pre-sentence reports (PSRs), specific types of community order, or work with sex offenders) have been looked at in detail - often called 'Quality and Effectiveness Inspections'; and (as with HMPS above) thematic inspections, where a given aspect of work is examined. Thematic inspections have usually occurred across several NPS local areas before recommendations were made to the home secretary about the wider issues arising, as well as advice being given to local areas. Interestingly, inspection reports have also contained comments about the linked performance of other agencies and of government departments. They have also contained 'commendations' whereby government, Probation Boards or other people have been made aware of good work and practice. All such reports are open to public scrutiny. As with inspectors of prisons, probation inspectors have sometimes found it necessary to disagree with ministers on given issues, including, e.g. at one time an attempt, in effect, to incorporate the probation service within HMPS.

THE PRISONS AND PROBATION OMBUDSMAN (PPO)

Like the Chief Inspectors of Prisons and Probation, the Prisons and Probation Ombudsman (PPO)[4] is now appointed by the Lord Chancellor (rather than, as previously, the home secretary). He or she investigates complaints from prisoners and offenders who are subject to various forms of community sentence, or about whom official reports that might affect a range of matters vis-à-vis the carrying out of their sentence (see further below) have been written. The PPO is wholly independent of the National Offender Management Service (NOMS), HM Prison Service (HMPS) and the National Probation Service (NPS). He or she is supported by a team of deputies, assistants, investigators and other staff.

The PPO also investigates deaths of prisoners[5] or residents of probation hostels or of people held in immigration detention centres. He or she can deal with complaints from:

- prisoners who are serving a prison sentence;
- prisoners who are on remand awaiting their trial or sentence;
- ex-prisoners who have complained about a problem that occurred whilst they were in prison;
- offenders who are subject to what is now the generic community order, principally forms of probation supervision, unpaid work and other associated requirements;[6]
- ex-prisoners who are on parole or licence and supervised by the NPS;
- people who have had a report written about them by the NPS.

Complaints must first have been raised and aired via the internal complaints system of either HMPS (known as 'requests and complaints' or 'R and C') or the NPS. The PPO will look at the complaint afresh and decide whether it has been dealt with fairly. If he or she upholds the complaint, recommendations are made to HMPS or the NPS as appropriate with a view to putting matters right.

---

[4] Formerly the Prisons Ombudsman. Since the inception of the role in 1994, the ombudsman has been Stephen Shaw, formerly director of the Prison Reform Trust.

[5] Often called 'deaths in custody', but that term is wider. It can include, e.g., deaths in police cells that are referred to the Independent Police Complaints Commission (IPPC).

[6] See further *Chapter 7*and for a full description of the generic community order *The Criminal Justice Act 2003: A Guide to the New Procedures and Sentencing* (2004), Gibson B, Waterside Press. For a general description of HMPS and the NPS see *Chapter 3*.

INDEPENDENT MONITORING BOARDS (IMBs)

Attached to and effectively inside every prison and immigration removal centre there is an Independent Monitoring Board (IMB) – a group of ordinary citizens voluntarily undertaking an independent public service role for some two to three days a month on average (though many IMB members contribute far more of their free time). IMBs have their origins in the visiting magistrates and boards of vistors which have been associated with prisons since the 19th century. IMBs and their members monitor the day-to-day life of their local prison or removal centre to which they are allocated in order to ensure that proper standards of care and decency are maintained. Each IMB meets regularly, usually at least once a month, and elects a chair and vice chair. IMB members also work as a team to raise any matters of concern with the prison governor or minister of state. Each year they produce an annual report that is published for the local community and other interested parties.

Members of IMBs have unhindered access to their local prison or immigration removal centre at any time and can talk to any prisoner or detainee as they choose, including out of the sight and hearing of members of staff if this is necessary. They might thus, e.g. as part of this free-ranging role, spend time on prison landings, in cells, in workshops, on farms, in recreation or prisoner association areas, healthcare centres, gymnasia, or with the prison chaplaincy. The IMB has a national secretariat[7] according to which:

> Board members also play an important role in dealing with problems inside the establishment. If a prisoner or detainee has an issue that he or she has been unable to resolve through the usual internal channels, he or she can put in a confidential request to see a member of the IMB. Problems might include concerns over lost property, visits from family or friends, special religious or cultural requirements, or even serious allegations such as bullying.

If a serious incident occurs at a particular establishment, such as a riot or a death in custody, IMB representatives may be called in to act as independent observers.

Qualities of IMB members

IMB members come from all types of background and walks of life and are of various ages. The IMB values 'the huge diversity of [its] members and the different combination of skills and experiences that each is able to bring'. It seeks to recruit members irrespective of any special qualifications and then provides the training that is needed to perform this role. But IMB recruitment materials do

---

[7] Based at Ashley House, Monck Street, Westminster SW1P 2BQ (adjacent to the offices of the Prisons and Probation Ombudsman); www.imb.gov.uk

indicate that the IMB particularly welcomes applications from people with energy and enthusiasm who are (paraphrased):

- open minded;
- caring;
- committed to diversity, equality and human rights; and
- good listeners.

It also seeks out the following skills:

- perseverance;
- integrity;
- willingness to take responsibility;
- ability to challenge;
- ability to maintain confidentiality;
- commitment;
- confidence;
- good teamwork skills; and
- effective communication skills.[8]

As well as a national secretariat, the IMB has a National Council, an elected body made up of nine IMB members and two co-opted members.

OTHER EXTERNAL SCRUTINY OF JUSTICE AGENCIES

Beyond the immediate network of MOJ-linked organizations, various other forms of external scrutiny or redress exist. These include the Criminal Cases Review Committee (CCRC) that looks at alleged instances of a miscarriage of justice and which has the authority to refer a case back to the Court of Appeal where it considers that a conviction is unsafe. In addition there are many charitable, reforming or campaign-based organizations that act as watchdogs, often using their own research, in relation to what public authorities are doing. In relation to the Criminal Justice System (CJS) these include long established and respected organizations such as the Howard League for Penal Reform, Prison Reform Trust (PRT) and National Association for the Care and Resettlement of Offenders (Nacro) and the legal and human-rights based groups JUSTICE and Liberty as well as countless smaller or specialist bodies. Certain of the advisory committees and other MOJ-sponsored bodies noted in *Appendix II* to this work also have an incidental if informal role in drawing the attention of the MOJ to matters that may require attention.

---

[8] This pro-active and relatively public search for IMB members would appear to contrast with an until now relatively low key (though sometimes public) search for magistrates.

Ultimately, it is Parliament and its Constitutional Affairs Committee (CAC) that provide democratic scrutiny of the MOJ under the constitutional arrangements noted in *Chapter 6*; whilst, as that chapter also notes, enhancements with regard to access to justice and freedom of information are also broader mechanisms of legitimacy and accountability.

CHAPTER 5

Law-Making and Legal Services

CHAPTER 5

Law-Making and Legal Services

The making of new laws is the constitutional responsibility of Parliament in the form of Acts of Parliament (often shortened to 'Act' and also known as 'statutes' or 'primary legislation'). Other laws that do not rank as Acts may also be made under the authority of an Act of Parliament, i.e. where the Act itself confers power to do so, usually to a secretary of state or minister of the Crown (as with statutory instruments or SIs)[1] or public authority (as with bye-laws). The outcome is known as 'legislation'. Where Parliament ('the legislature') has delegated its responsibility to a minister, etc. the resulting legislation is known as 'delegated legislation' or 'secondary legislation'. Delegated legislation must fall within the power granted by the parent Act, a doctrine known as *intra vires*.

Various MOJ functions are to the fore in this process, particularly those of a constitutional nature and with regard to the legislative or 'law-making' process as a whole whether relating to the constitution, civil and criminal justice, family law or other incidents of MOJ responsibility. These include the Office for Criminal Justice Reform (below). Other government departments sponsor their own legislation but where there are overlapping interests cross-departmental arrangements exist of the kind noted in *Chapter 1* under *Partnership*.

Naturally both legal processes and legislation can often be complex matters. Hence also an MOJ responsibility exists to ensure that people have access to courts and tribunals and, according to their circumstances and situation, the legal or other services that will enable them to obtain justice. This is widely spoken of as 'access to justice'. The chapter also looks at the arrangements that exist in this regard, including in relation to legal services and legal aid. It also looks at the role and responsibilities of the attorney general who heads the law officers and whose office is a constituent part of the trilateral group or 'special relationship' encompassing the MOJ, Home Office and Office of the Attorney General referred to in *Chapter 1* – a role that has attracted controversy in modern times.

ACCESS TO JUSTICE

In its key first day publication *Justice: A New Approach*,[2] the MOJ made the resounding promise, 'We will provide access to justice for all'. It also asserts that:

---

[1] To further compound terminology SIs and bye-laws may each be styled 'regulations', but Acts may also contain regulations, particularly, e.g. in a schedule to an Act.

[2] (2007); Ministry of Justice.

An effective justice system is not just about the courts and the judges: it concerns the extent to which the public has access to that system. Access depends on understanding one's rights and knowing how to go about enforcing them. Too many people still do not know where to turn, or are too confused, intimidated or indeed frightened to access the justice system. This is often the case for the people in the greatest need.

According to the MOJ, access to justice means making sure that people, particularly those who are the most vulnerable and disadvantaged in society, are able to obtain the help, advice and support that they need. It points out that early, quick and easily understood information, e.g. on debt, welfare or housing can often prevent problems spiralling out of control:

But if problems do escalate, we must encourage people, where appropriate, to look for alternatives to court.[3] In family justice, for instance we must continue to give the strongest possible encouragement to mediation so that families can resolve their disputes without the distress that court can bring. In civil justice we will promote alternatives where the expense and formality of a court hearing is not required, including making use of justice online … Since the Attlee government [of 1945-51] introduced legal aid nearly 60 years ago, it has provided millions of people with advice, support and representation – many of whom would have been otherwise denied access to justice because they could not have afforded to pay. Free access to justice for those who need legal aid is as integral to the Welfare State as the NHS or state education. Our legal aid system is the best funded in the world, but we must ensure that the system is sustainable for the future and that it continues to provide protection for the most vulnerable. This means reforming the way that legal aid is provided in order that expensive criminal cases do not draw invaluable support away from civil or family aid, where it is often needed most.

The Legal Services Commission (LSC)

The LSC is responsible for looking after legal aid in England and Wales. It also seeks to ensure that people can obtain the information, advice and legal help they need to deal with a wide range of problems. It works in partnership with solicitors and the voluntary sector in order to achieve this, including in relation to people in need. The LSC vision includes making sure 'that clients can access the help they need to address their problems'. The LSC runs the Legal Aid Scheme (below) which the LSC notes 'safeguards some of society's most vulnerable and disadvantaged people' and it assists some two million people a year to deal with their legal problems. The LSC has quality standards that professional and other advisers must meet and who are then entitled to display a Quality Mark.

---

[3] See the general note on alternative dispute resolution (ADR) procedures in *Chapter 8*.

Correspondingly, the MOJ asserts that it will work with the LSC to ensure that legal aid provides access to justice to help people in need of legal advice and representation who would not otherwise be able to afford it, including in relation to debt, divorce, housing disputes and other situations where they need to safeguard their rights. According to the MOJ, more people nowadays receive legal assistance through the LSC than at any time since 2000, the number of individual acts of assistance having risen since 2002 by more than a third, from 595,000 to around 800,000 in 2007.

Legal aid

According to the LSC, legal aid helps to ensure access to justice by providing high quality advice, information and representation to people who would not otherwise be able to afford it, meaning that clients can protect their rights by:

- taking early advice;
- being able to defend themselves if accused of a crime; and
- taking a case to court when this is the best way to resolve a dispute.

According to the MOJ,[4] there is strong evidence that the provision of good early legal advice helps to prevent relatively simple civil legal issues spiralling into more serious, numerous and complex problems. It claims that its own investigations show that people can tend to suffer 'clusters of problems', e.g. someone with a state benefits problem may also need advice on debt, leading to a need for legal advice to bridge more than one area of law:

> To meet the needs of those with multiple problems, we will provide access to advice across the key categories of social welfare law, together with family advice. The LSC will jointly commission services at a local level, primarily with local authorities. This will mean that services directly meet the needs of local people. It will also mean that providers deliver services where clients need them and not where they have historically been based, shortening travel times and improving access.

The MOJ also points to the fact that legal aid is important, not just for protecting people who have been arrested and other defendants, but also because it can assist in resolving cases early, through measures such as fixed penalty notices and conditional cautions at a police station; and that for more serious and complex matters where prosecution and a hearing *are* necessary, high quality publicly-funded defence services are a key part of providing a speedy, effective Criminal Justice System (CJS) 'which commands public confidence, minimises the burden on victims and witnesses and delivers justice for all':

---

[4] Legal aid leaflet (2007). Other quotes in this section are also taken from that leaflet.

If a problem does get to court, across all jurisdictions we must do all we can to speed up, simplify and explain the process. In magistrates' courts the Simple, Speedy, Summary programme has put an onus on the courts to reduce unnecessary hearings and to progress cases faster. In family justice we will work to reduce delays in care cases, to reduce the trauma and distress that can be caused by unnecessarily long proceedings ... We must ensure that people have the confidence as well as the understanding to access justice ... that they will receive the necessary support throughout the process. In particular, we must ensure that victims and witnesses are given the support they need when they attend court, to not feel threatened, to give their best evidence and to deal with any negative effects of their case ... so that ... they feel proud to perform their civic duty and to contribute to the pursuit of justice, and that their commitment is recognised by the justice system and the community at large[5] ... We will also ensure that we embrace equality and remove disproportionality across the justice system. We know, for example, that women with histories of violence and abuse and some minority ethnic groups are over-represented in the CJS.

The MOJ also points out that 'to deny access is to deny justice'; and that different approaches are needed, e.g. for different groups of people facing such problems, so as to ensure that they are treated equally. It thus promises that it 'will:

- provide access to advice, at the point of need and at the earliest possible opportunity, to help people resolve their disputes earlier;
- promote alternatives to court, such as mediation, that avoid the formality, cost and distress that can be a feature of court hearings;
- work with the Legal Services Commission on planned reform of the legal aid system, so that it is fair to the vulnerable, fair to taxpayers, fair to defendants, and fair to practitioners;
- ensure that courts are more open and that judicial decisions are better understood;
- introduce simpler processes across all jurisdictions [so that] if a problem gets to court, the court processes are faster [and] more efficient;
- promote specialist support services – encouraging people to come forward in the first instance, and then provide support throughout the process; and
- deliver interventions for offenders[6] according to their needs to reduce re-offending.'

Public Defender Service (PDS)
The PDS describes itself as 'the first salaried criminal provider in England and Wales', i.e. for accused people.[7] There are four PDS offices in England and Wales

---

[5] See further with regard to victims and witnesses in *Chapter 8*.

[6] See, generally, *Chapter 7, Sentencing Policy and Guidelines*.

[7] An exact quote. See www.legalservices.gov.uk/criminal/pds

at Cheltenham, Darlington, Pontypridd and Swansea. The LSC (above) directly employs a PDS staff of solicitors, accredited representatives and administrators. The PDS then provides independent advice, assistance and representation on criminal matters, PDS lawyers being available 24 hours a day, seven days a week to: give advice to people in custody; represent clients in magistrates' courts, Crown Courts and the higher courts where necessary. There is a PDS code of conduct which all PDS employees must observe, including to ensure independence from the LSC.

Community Legal Service Direct (CLSD)

Community Legal Service Direct is a free and confidential advice service paid for by legal aid where people, including those on a low income or state benefits can telephone for independent advice about debt, education, benefits and tax credits, employment and housing problems.[8]

Legal Services Act 2007

An embryonic and sometimes controversial Legal Services Act 2007 (LSA) introduces an innovative approach to the delivery of legal services whereby lawyers will be provided via mixed professional practices, companies or banks as well as front line regulators and a disciplinary framework[9] under the auspices of a new Legal Services Board (predictably to be appointed jointly by the Lord Chancellor and Lord Chief Justice) and an Office of Legal Complaints.

These developments occur against an equally controversial background in which, so some commentators argue, there have been increasing constraints on legal aid budgets, concerns about lawyers being asked to take on more *pro bono* (non-remunerative) work and the departure from certain unprofitable specialist areas of work, particularly those linked to more vulnerable and less well off people, by significant numbers of firms of solicitors who formerly had longstanding practices in such fields.

Some people have concerns about these developments that might seem to be at odds with MOJ assurances about more universal access to justice; whilst others see them as a welcome aspect of democratising legal services, that may also enhance access to justice in the longer term by being more market-responsive.

THE OFFICE FOR CRIMINAL JUSTICE REFORM (OCJR)

The OCJR was established in 2004 as an integral part of a major government review of the ability of the Criminal Justice System (CJS) to deliver core Public

---

[8]   0845 345 4 345; see www.clsdirect.org.uk
[9]   There is currently a Legal Services Ombudsman: see www.olso.org

Service Agreement targets,[10] the OCJR's main purpose being to drive forward improvements in the CJS. It is a cross-departmental arrangement that supports all criminal justice departments and agencies in working together to provide an improved service to the public. It reports to ministers in the MOJ (now the lead-agency, post-Home Office split of 2007), Home Office and the Office of the Attorney General (below). The OCJR's stated objectives are 'to deliver the National Criminal Justice Board's (NCJB's) vision of what the Criminal Justice System (CJS) will look like in 2008'. This states that by then:

- the public will have confidence that the CJS is effective and that it serves all communities fairly;
- victims and witnesses will receive a consistently high standard of service from all criminal justice agencies;
- the CJS will bring more offences to justice through a more modern and efficient justice system;
- rigorous enforcement will revolutionise compliance with sentences and orders of the court; and
- criminal justice will be a joined-up, modern and well-run service, and an excellent place to work for people from all backgrounds.

This vision rests on various public service agreements designed to improve the delivery of justice across a similar timescale, e.g. by increasing the number of crimes for which an offender is brought to justice, reassuring the public, reducing the fear of crime and anti-social behaviour, and building confidence in the CJS without compromising fairness.[11]

THE ATTORNEY GENERAL

The role of the attorney general (AG) is some five centuries old. The AG is the Crown's chief law officer who tenders his or her advice in complex situation to the Government, to which he or she is chief legal adviser. He or she also supervises each of the two main public prosecuting agencies in England and Wales, the Crown Prosecution Service (CPS) and the Serious Fraud Office (SFO), including with regard to decisions whether or not to prosecute someone in serious cases such as murder and those involving terrorism. Certain prosecutions require his or her consent, or fiat, as it is called. There is also a broad public

---

[10] This formalised and built on the work of its predecessor, the Criminal Justice Group.
[11] However all such agreements would, in so far as they concern targets, now appear to require examination in the light of an announcement by prime minister Gordon Brown on 17 July 2007 that many government targets would be dispensed with or revised. Those referable, e.g. to 'fear of crime' were specifically mentioned in this regard.

interest duty, one example of which is that of appeal to the Court of Appeal against what the AG considers to be certain 'unduly lenient sentences'. This power has been gradually extended in its scope. More generally, the AG is often described as the guardian of the public interest and has a wide discretion to intervene as an external party in court proceedings or processes. Neither the AG nor the Office of the Attorney General is part of the MOJ, but it is closely allied as a partner within the key, trilateral arrangement/'special relationship' between the AG, Lord Chancellor and home secretary, referred to in *Chapter 1*.

The AG's responsibilities evolved gradually over the centuries and without any specific or targeted consideration of their overall constitutional implications. The complexity of the role has attracted much public comment around several issues in modern times, most notably the position of the AG as:

- chief legal adviser to the government; and
- as guardian of the public interest.

These arose from a number of events but are most strongly associated with the nature and legality of advice given by the AG to the Government concerning the legality of the Iraq War, interventions whereby a long-running criminal investigation into corruption at BAE systems was ended in the national interest, and a degree of prevarication concerning who would or should take the final decision for or against prosecution in relation to the 2006-7 cash for honours investigation that directly concerned Number Ten Downing Street. Hence assurances by Government in the MOJ Green Paper, *The Governance of Britain*[12] that it is fully committed to enhancing public confidence and trust. The MOJ

> will therefore publish a consultation document … which considers possible ways of alleviating these conflicts (or the appearance of them) and invites comments. The Government looks forward in particular to the report of the Constitutional Affairs Select Committee of the House of Commons, and will study [it] carefully … The AG will continue to exercise statutory superintendence functions over the prosecution authorities throughout this consultation exercise. The trilateral arrangements for the criminal justice system involving a partnership of the home secretary, secretary of state for justice [and Lord Chancellor] and the AG will continue. The position of Her Majesty's Attorney General as legal adviser to the Crown remains unchanged.

Ahead of any such changes, on taking up her appointment as attorney general in 2007, Baroness Scotland,[13] announced that she would no longer be involved in a range of sensitive areas. As already indicated, the role is to be specifically examined within the consultations triggered by *The Governance of Britain*.

---

12 (2007) Cm 7170.
13 The UK's first woman AG and also the first black AG.

CHAPTER 6

Constitutional Affairs
and Human Rights

CHAPTER 6

Constitutional Affairs and Human Rights

As explained at the very start of this book, the new Ministry of Justice (MOJ) arose from a reshaping and extension of the former Department of Constitutional Affairs (DCA). As that former name implies, constitutional matters were central to its responsibilities, as they were part of the remit of the earlier Lord Chancellor's Department (LCD). Justice has always been regarded as integral to constitutional affairs even though from time to time there may have been a role for – or overlap of responsibilities with – other government departments such as the Home Office. In terms of the name MOJ, the relationship between 'justice' and the 'constitution' has been inverted. Whatever may lie in a name, the creation of the MOJ triggered a fresh interest in constitutional issues.

THE BRITISH CONSTITUTION

The UK is unique amongst modern western-style democracies in relying on an *unwritten* constitution. That constitution is an amalgam of common law, legislation, convention and works of authority (as to the last of which, see further below under the heading *High Constitutional Principle*). Its genesis goes back many hundreds of years as noted in the summary in *Appendix I* to this work, which sets out the main stages of constitutional development. As noted in the Green Paper, *The Governance of Britain*:[1]

> In Britain our constitution has evolved organically to renew the relationship between government and citizen, and to respond to the challenges we have faced as a nation. It is from this constant evolution that we draw strength.

The Constitutional Affairs Committee
The Constitutional Affairs Committee is the Parliamentary committee which scrutinises the work of the MOJ across all its responsibilities. Periodically, also, that committee investigates the MOJ's work on freedom of information (below). In one of its sittings soon after the creation of the MOJ it heard from the Lord Chief Justice, Lord Phillips of Worth Matravers, concerning issues arising from the new inter-agency nature of the MOJ and the need for satisfactory assurances concerning judicial independence (*Chapter 3*).

---

[1] Cm 7170. For the Foreword, Executive Summary and Introduction see *Appendix IV* to this work. The complete version is available at www.justice.gov.uk

Stamping out myths and moving towards a written constitution

In popular culture, such iconic events as Magna Carta (1215) or the Declaration of Rights (1689) and its accompanying Glorious Revolution frequently serve as reference points for rights and freedoms. But closer scrutiny or a search for specific detail can prove frustrating. Certain constitutional matters and key reference points for the UK constitution may be generally agreed upon, but constitutional law, even the exact meaning of 'constitutional', can be a matter of debate, even amongst experts. Hence many commentators would now appear to accept that the lack of a clear, rational, embedded and accessible code covering constitutional matters represents a major defect in these arrangements. The publication by the MOJ in 2007 of the Green Paper, *The Governance of Britain*,[2] inviting views on a range of matters, including whether there might better be a *written* constitution, can thus be viewed as a highly significant development. This is driven not just by a commitment by New Labour to a programme of constitutional reform,[3] but by a sense that certain constitutional arrangements fall short of international standards, including those typified by the European Convention On Human Rights (ECHR). Particularly since its incorporation into UK law by the Human Rights Act 1998, the ECHR is now in fact part of the legal foundation on which the UK constitution rests.

There are yet wider forces at work. There have been moves to establish a Europe-wide constitution that could, unless the UK acts quickly, begin to overshadow more localised, purely national initiatives. It is ironic, perhaps, that in European Union debates the fact that the UK has 'only an unwritten constitution' has been put forward by UK representatives as a reason why the UK might be allowed certain exemptions from such a Europe-wide measure. Whilst some people may still pride themselves on protecting the UK's idiosyncratic approach to constitutional matters, it has for others become obvious in modern times that UK arrangements, for all their sometimes outward grandeur, fine language and explanation, lack transparency, accountability and are ultimately unsustainable in the modern world.

These included the position of the Lord Chancellor, no less (formerly an anomalous role in relation to each of the three separate arms of state: see next section), a defect cured when a number of associated concerns were also answered by provisions contained in the Constitutional Reform Act 2005: see, particularly, *Chapters 3* and *9*); and that of the attorney general (*Chapter 4*). Along with mythical explanations, idiosyncratic ways of doing things can serve to mask flaws in what ought to be impregnable constitutional safeguards.

---

[2] See previous footnote.
[3] That stems from its election manifesto of 1997.

HIGH CONSTITUTIONAL PRINCIPLE

Central to constitutional matters sit two historic doctrines:

- the supremacy of Parliament; and
- the separation of powers.

The Government's stance on the future of the UK Constitution is encapsulated in the MOJ Green Paper, *The Governance of Britain:*

> In parallel to consideration of the articulation of the rights of each citizen is the articulation of our constitution. Constitutions should allow the citizen to understand and fully engage with the state and state institutions. The vast majority of countries have codified, written and embedded constitutions. The UK has not. Instead, the British constitution has four principal sources – statute law, common law, conventions and works of authority, such as those of Walter Bagehot and A. V. Dicey – among which under the doctrine of parliamentary sovereignty, statute law is pre-eminent … Partly by virtue of the political stability since the end of the 17th century, there has been no key event that has led to the need for one document setting out the rules on issues such as the length of parliamentary terms, the method of election to the House of Commons and appointment to the House of Lords, the powers of the judiciary, the powers of the devolved authorities, and the method whereby Bills become law … Today, we have to ensure that our country remains a cohesive, confident society in dealing with the challenges of the 21st century. Previous sections of this document have discussed the need to provide a clearer articulation of British values, and greater clarity about the nature of British citizenship. But there is now a growing recognition of the need to clarify not just what it means to be British, but what it means to be the United Kingdom. This might in time lead to a concordat[4] between the executive and Parliament or a written constitution.

The doctrine of the separation of powers has already been referred to in *Chapter 2* when looking at the independence of the judiciary. It rests on the idea that for western-style democracy to remain at all viable, people who hold and exercise power must operate within a system of checks and balances, since ultimately, so wisdom would have it, power tends to corrupt.[5] In the extreme then, the doctrine is a counterweight to abuse, oppression and ultimately tyranny. It is of quite ancient origin and can be traced in its various forms to, e.g. the Greek philosopher Aristotle who wrote that the fairest political system was one in which power was shared between the monarchy, aristocracy, and citizens. John Locke's 17th century adaptation urged that government should be split into

---

[4] Note also 'The Concordat' already established with the judiciary: *Chapter 3.*
[5] Just as wisdom has it that absolute power corrupts absolutely.

two parts: an executive to administer the country and a legislature to make laws and oversee and, if need be, withdraw, amend or replace them.

Modern-day versions of the doctrine perhaps owe more to the writings of the French political theorist, Charles de Montesquieu (1689-1755) who concentrated on the addition of a third estate, the judiciary, whose role, among other things, included the resolution of disputes between the first two parties as to what the law meant, the extent of the powers that it conveyed, and containing tendencies to excess.[6] This led to the basic premise that the legislature (or Parliament) must operate independently of the executive (or Government of the day) and that the judiciary and supporting legal system should also operate independently of either of the first two and without any particular bias, interference, or pressure being applied. In other words, the judiciary were to be the constitutional safeguard against the descent that would inevitably occur, sooner or later, if the Government and Parliament were left to their own devices; whilst, e.g. citizens might challenge the Government through their elected representatives.[7] As already noted, in the UK this protection is now reinforced by the Constitutional Reform Act 2005 and Human Rights Act 1998.

Such issues have become intertwined with perceived domination of the UK legislature by the executive, extensive delegated or regulatory powers[8] and the correspondingly weakened authority of Parliament, leading to questions in *The Governance of Britain* around 'reinvigorating democracy' and calls for a more inclusive approach. Constitutional issues arise in relation to the creation of the MOJ itself of course: especially whether the judiciary is now sufficiently independent of the executive when, effectively, housed under the same umbrella as NOMS (*Chapter 3*) and legal services (*Chapter 5*). There is a similar dilemma in relation to tribunals. There is also always the prospect that judges or tribunal members might find themselves dealing with court-related or tribunal-related matters to which the MOJ is a party[9] or in which the MOJ or its partners (*Chapter 1*) have a pressing interest vis-à-vis the outcome; with the problems for fairness (including justice being seen to be done) that this entails. Many commentators sense that this makes the judiciary susceptible to underlying pressures, political, financial and otherwise – or at least to the offshoots or repercussions of executive decisions. This seems to go well beyond the scope of the kind of practical

---

[6] *The Spirit of the Laws* (1752).

[7] This theory ignores the historically non-democratic and formerly self-perpetuating and partially reformed House of Lords, now further addressed in *The Governance of Britain*.

[8] Sometimes described as 'Henry VIII' clauses or 'skeleton Acts'; of which the Criminal Justice Act 2003 can be suggested as a prime, modern-day, example.

[9] E.g. in a high profile case in 2007, the Lord Chancellor indicated that he was considering an appeal against a partly human rights-based tribunal decision not to deport the man who in 1995 as a juvenile (born in Italy) killed the headteacher Philip Lawrence.

safeguards that have already been suggested by the MOJ such as 'ring fencing' of court and judicial budgets. The problem may be more one of subtle forms of ambushing by the other agencies. There is an analogous if not so obvious problem with cross-justice department involvements (*Chapter 1*) or cross-agency inspections (*Chapter 4*).

The judiciary – headed by the Lord Chief Justice (*Chapter 2*) – has proved hardy and resilient when defending its role. It has frequently warned against the making of questionable laws, or held up the actions of the executive to scrutiny, including via the legal process known as judicial review of executive action (often shortened to 'judicial review'). Where statute gives a minister or other public officer a discretion, then he or she must not only exercise it by taking relevant considerations into account and discounting irrelevant considerations, but must do so within the law of the land, legally, reasonably, fairly and proportionately. It was the Human Rights Act 1998 (HRA) that introduced this latter strand – the principle of proportionality – that now applies both to courts and ministers, etc. Governments or ministers have occasionally appeared to speak out of turn in criticising the judiciary as 'obstructive' or 'unrealistic' - as where ministers have been called to account in relation to detention without trial and control orders, both of which have been held to be unlawful[10] - but this chink in the armour of the doctrine of the separation of powers has been short lived, glossed over and to an extent repaired. Even former prime minister Tony Blair and former home secretary Dr John Reid at times hinted at the 'inconvenience' of the 1998 Act or the way it was being interpreted by the judiciary, without, as they saw it, a sufficient balancing of the interests of the state (or proportionality). This caused the then Lord Chancellor, Lord Falconer to intervene on one occasion to 'reinterpret' such remarks from a less political perspective.

Judges as law-makers

Both the legislature and the judges 'make law', but the latter not in the legislative sense. Rather, it is because judges are responsible for the interpretation of the law, a task which can sometimes be viewed as being carried out more creatively or imaginatively than Parliament envisaged, albeit that the judges would always say that they thereby merely discover the intentions of Parliament. This they do following well-rehearsed rules and avenues of interpretation. Judges also declare the common law that, in the past, may have involved the creation of criminal offences.[11] Whatever the overlap between Parliament and the judiciary in terms

---

[10] Detention without trial outside of the terms of the Police and Criminal Evidence Act 1984 (PACE) or other legislation is unlawful; control orders (re terrorist suspects) also if human rights are over-ridden, e.g. the right to liberty; to a private and family life.

[11] There is a potentially endless debate about whether judges make law or not, due to the flexibility of the common law. It is uncertain whether, post-ECHR, due to a greater need

of their respective functions, the judges have always deferred to the express authority of Parliament. It is generally accepted that, however bad or confusing legislative provisions may be, the judiciary cannot invalidate Acts of Parliament. But they do, under the HRA 1998, have the authority to declare secondary legislation (variously described as statutory instruments (SIs) or delegated legislation) invalid and primary legislation (statutes, also known as Acts of Parliament: *Chapter 5*) incompatible with the ECHR. The latter kind of declaration invokes a process whereby a responsible minister must consider whether amending legislation is needed or appropriate.

THE EUROPEAN CONVENTION ON HUMAN RIGHTS

The Human Rights Act 1998 (HRA 1998) came into force in October 2000 having been hailed as one of the most important pieces of constitutional legislation in UK history. The HRA was a commitment of the New Labour Government that took up office in 1997. The development was announced in a Green Paper, *Bringing Rights Home*. The then Lord Chancellor Derry Irvine was at the forefront of these events and much was made by him of the merits of at last signing up to the full rigour of the ECHR (below).[12] Since the HRA 1998, the scope for self-determination by the UK (or by the same token other member countries of the European Union who have signed up to the ECHR) is to an extent proscribed by the ECHR. Discussion of whether there should be a UK written constitution inevitably also raises questions as to whether that constitution would replace, incorporate or stand alongside the 1998 Act.[13]

Human rights as a constitutional responsibility

It is perhaps hardly surprising then that the MOJ categorises human rights as one of several areas that fall within its 'constitutional' responsibilities – though it appears to do so without giving human rights any special priority.[14] Neither, e.g. are human rights included within the more basic of the key aims noted at the MOJ web-site and reproduced in *Chapter 1* (any more than protecting the judiciary is). In retrospect, the 1998 Act that New Labour was initially so keen to promote came at times to be regarded by that Government and sections of the

---

for certainty and a bar on retrospective liability, judges can create offences (if they could before or not). The most striking example of a common law offence is murder.

[12] The background to the ECHR and the Human Rights Act 1998 Act are set out in *Human Rights and the Courts: Bringing Justice Home* (1999), Ashcroft P *et al*, Waterside Press.

[13] Whichever route is chosen, the UK cannot now ordinarily depart from the articles of the ECHR – short, it seems, of leaving the European Union; although it can derogate from it on the grounds of national security. Whenever a state does so, it risks losing face.

[14] The MOJ web-site has an information page and other links devoted to human rights.

media as an impediment or obstacle and its reputation undoubtedly suffered thereby, especially if a suspect or offender appeared to gain from ECHR protection in a situation where a victim of crime may have felt less well-served. As a result the ECHR suffered some quite unjustified and often ill-informed criticism from certain quarters, including sections of the tabloid press, especially the *Sun* newspaper, which has waged a sustained and rancorous campaign for its repeal. Prior to the MOJ and *The Governance of Britain*, the DCA had already, in 2006, commenced a 'Review of the Implementation of the Human Rights Act'.

Human rights summarised
The main rights protected by the ECHR and enshrined in the HRA 1998 are:

- Article 2 Right to life;
- Article 3 Prohibition of torture;
- Article 4 Prohibition of slavery and forced labour;
- Article 5 Right to liberty and security;
- Article 6 Right to a fair trial;
- Article 7 No punishment without law;
- Article 8 Right to respect for private and family life;
- Article 9 Freedom of thought, conscience and religion;
- Article 10 Freedom of expression;
- Article 11 Freedom of assembly and association;
- Article 12 Right to marry;
- Article 14 Prohibition of discrimination;[15]
- Protocol 1, Article 1 Protection of property;
- Protocol 1, Article 2 Right to education; and
- Protocol 1, Article 3 Right to free elections.

Other Protocols have seen the abolition of the death penalty in those countries, including the UK, that have signed up to and fully ratified them: Protocols 6 (no peacetime executions); and the more recent Protocol 13 (no executions at any time). Such matters may still require ratification by the state which signs up to them. Hence, e.g. the last vestiges of the death penalty only really disappeared from the UK in 2004 when Parliament ratified Protocol 13. Anecdotally, it seems to be Articles 5 (liberty and security), 6 (fair trial) and 8 (private and family life) that have been in the news as a mainstay of day-to-day court-based challenges, but so have Article 3 (torture), Article 9 (freedom of thought, etc.), Article 10 (freedom of expression) and Article 11 (freedom of assembly, etc.), variously, e.g. in relation to terrorism, UK involvement in extraordinary rendition, and political

---

[15] This is not a right or protection in the ordinary sense, but a reinforcement of rights in other articles of the ECHR which must be applied without discrimination.

demonstrations.[16] The ECHR is underpinned by European jurisprudence of which the doctrine of proportionality is perhaps the foremost, whereby rights in the convention must be applied in a balanced way taking account of state and private interests, and except where they are absolute, as e.g. is the right against torture.[17] Despite the bad press that has been given to the HRA 1998 by sections of the media, the Government and MOJ are committed to it and its protection, whether as it presently exists or within some new Bill of Rights and Duties of the state and its citizens or a written constitution as is clear from the Green Paper, *The Governance of Britain*, further mentioned in the next section:

> We will uphold peoples' human, information and democratic rights. A just society is one in which basic freedoms not only exist but are fully protected ... It is a society which accepts we are all equal and we are all entitled to have our individual freedoms protected. Upholding rights relies on ensuring there is an understanding of rights, knowledge of when they are being infringed and effective mechanisms in place by which they can meaningfully be enforced ... [It] is not about focusing on or protecting one group in society; it is about providing a practical framework to protect all our freedoms. The HRA 1998 operates on a practical as well as an ideological level. It protects us as individuals, whilst defending our values as a society. Rights are the property of the community. They are for all of us, not simply reserved for the lawyer or for minorities ... Our commitment to upholding rights means we must protect and promote the HRA 1998. We must start from an early age, embedding these values in our young people as part of their education. We will continue to argue that human rights and human rights legislation [are] both necessary and effective, constitutionally compatible, and morally appropriate. We will continue to argue that human rights reflect both common values and common sense.

THE GOVERNANCE OF BRITAIN

In their Foreword to *The Governance of Britain*, prime minister Gordon Brown and Lord Chancellor Jack Straw set out their joint vision for the future:

---

[16] It is interesting, e.g. that the MOJ, which is expressly committed to a more democratic and inclusive approach, has indicated that it will review bans on such demonstrations (long part of a proud tradition that has sometimes been dubbed Britain's 'radical heritage'). How, e.g. should it respond to the case of Brian Haw, a long-term demonstrator outside the Houses of Parliament against the Iraq War (as it was, now, it seems, a 'conflict') who managed to partially overturn a modern-day ban on demonstrations within one mile of Parliament, on a legal technicality, thus almost passing into folk lore? Unable to use all his placards, some were removed to the nearby Tate Gallery and displayed as part of an exhibition, 'State Britain'! On protest generally, see *Chapter 5* of *The New Home Office*.

[17] Again, see *Human Rights and the Courts* noted in an earlier footnote.

Our constitutional arrangements fundamentally underpin how we function as a nation. The nature of the relationship the Government has with its citizens, the credibility of our institutions, and the rights and responsibilities of citizens all determine the health of our democracy.[18]

They go on to note that in 1997 the Government embarked on a major programme of constitutional change whereby:

- power was devolved away from Westminster;
- fundamental rights were enshrined in the HRA 1998 (above);
- freedom of information was introduced (below); and
- the Government completed the first stage of a reformed House of Lords (see the note in *Chapter 2*).

They also urge that there is a need to address two 'fundamental questions:

- how should we hold [those who possess] power accountable; and
- how should we uphold and enhance the rights and responsibilities of citizens.'

The tenor of the Green Paper can be characterised by saying that it is about 'new relationships', a 'national conversation', 'constitutional renewal', 'renewing trust' and 'reinvigorating democracy' – and the document also emphasises the need to move forward quickly. It would be impossible here to convey all the questions that it raises, or their nuances, so what follows concentrates on the more justice-oriented aspects of a sweeping agenda of questions and suggestions.

Bill of Rights and Duties

The Green Paper talks of a possible Bill of Rights and Duties that could

... provide explicit recognition that human rights come with responsibilities and must be exercised in a way that respects the human rights of others. It would build on the basic principles of the HRA 1998, but make explicit the way in which a democratic society's rights have to be balanced by obligations. The Government itself recognised, in its review last year of the implementation of the HRA 1998 the importance which must attach to public safety and ensuring that Government agencies accord appropriate priority to protection of the public when balancing rights. A Bill of Rights and Duties might provide a means of giving greater clarity and legislative force to this commitment. However, a framework of civic responsibilities – were it to be given legislative force – would need to avoid encroaching upon personal freedoms and civil liberties which have been hard won over centuries of our history ... It is clear that neither a Bill of Rights and Duties nor a written constitution could come into being except over an extended period of time, through extensive and wide consultation,

---

[18] The Foreword is reproduced in full within *Appendix IV* to this work.

and not without broad consensus upon the values upon which they were based and the rights and responsibilities which derived from them. The process of national debate through which the Government proposes to develop a British statement of values provides an opportunity to begin exploring the issues that would need to be considered. But this can only be considered as the start of a much longer process. The fundamental and constitutional nature of the guarantees provided in such instruments – as 50 years' experience of the ECHR has demonstrated – require both government and Parliament to proceed with caution.

National identity[19]

According to the MOJ, national identity is founded in the values we hold in common, and manifested through our history and our institutions. If we are to forge the shared sense of national purpose we need to meet the economic and social challenges ahead, UK institutions must reflect these values. The programme of constitutional reform as set out in *The Governance of Britain* seeks to meet that objective by renewing UK democracy. This task does not fall to government alone, but to all citizens of the UK – and the discussion now begins.

Together with the creation of the MOJ, prime minister Gordon Brown's 'politics of engagement' might raise fresh hopes for those who would prefer a more inclusive society of citizens who believe that they can make a difference.

The state and the citizen

Whilst much of what has been talked about is of a high political nature, matters, e.g. concerning the role of the monarchy, Parliament, Government and reform of the House of Lords, there has also been mention of a written constitution that would formalise such matters as the separation of powers (above) and set out the rights of citizens to challenge the actions or intentions of the state. It is a huge undertaking that Gordon Brown has already indicated may take some years and that may not all be completed in one go – but there is evidently a new commitment to such ideas and the possibility that, subject to wide consultation, a written constitution might be arrived at. Hence his proposals – a road map - for 'a new constitutional settlement that entrusts more power to the British people', 'reinvigorates democracy' and 'improves direct democracy' whilst reducing the power of the prime minister and providing a new basis for the relationship between citizens and the state.

An important and significant part of that new relationship would be a reform of the use of the Royal prerogative:

---

[19] Mention of the word 'identity' immediately triggers thoughts of Home Office moves to map people's identities through identity cards, the growth of linked databases, crime and immigration issues (re which, of course, the MOJ is a crime reduction and crime prevention partner): and see further the companion to this work, *The New Home Office.*

For centuries [prime ministers] have exercised authority in the name of the monarchy without the people or their elected representatives being consulted ... I now propose that in twelve important areas ... the prime minister and executive should surrender or limit their powers, the exclusive exercise of which ... should have no place in a modern democracy.

As further explained in *The Governance of Britain*, these matters concerning which there would be new and better Parliamentary or other appropriate scrutiny and a greater degree of Parliamentary oversight concern powers to:

- declare war;
- ask for the dissolution of or recall of Parliament;
- ratify international treaties;
- make senior public appointments;
- select bishops;
- help in the appointment of judges;
- set rules in relation to the civil service;
- direct prosecutors in criminal cases;
- make rules about pardons with regard to criminal sentences; and
- restrict Parliamentary oversight of the intelligence services.

The Lord Chancellor and MOJ would be charged with overseeing the development of these matters. The Green Paper includes promises to review the right to protest in the proximity of the Houses of Parliament contained in the Serious and Organized Crime and Police Act 2005.[20] As already noted, in looking at those constitutional arrangements that 'underpin how we function as a nation' it describes the nature of the relationship between government and citizens, the accountability of UK institutions, and the rights and responsibilities of everyone in Britain that together determine the health of UK democracy. Centrally, its raises two fundamental questions, i.e. (paraphrased):

- how power can be held accountable; and
- how the rights and responsibilities of citizens can be balanced with this.

There are also proposals to engage people in a discussion on citizenship and what have been styled 'British values' via a series of events across the UK so as 'to gain as much input as possible' as already indicated in the section on *Human rights*, above. The Government and MOJ also describe the Freedom of

---

[20] For further restrictions on citizens and wide-ranging police powers in response to terrorism or the fear of terrorism in the wake of September 11 and July 7 and subsequent security threats, see the companion to this work, *The New Home Office*.

Information Act 2000 (below) as 'one of the greatest reforms for which this [the Labour party] will rightly be remembered' adding that:

> Before 1997, governments were not nearly open enough. The culture was one of non-disclosure. There was the expectation and an acceptance that governments in this country should govern, but not govern openly ... This Government has opened up Whitehall and beyond in ways unimagined, unattempted and unrealised by any previous government in the UK. With a culture of openness in government and direct access to information will come better government and greater confidence. By seeing the factual basis on which decisions are made, the citizen can hold the public authority more fully to account. Giving people the power of information is central to the aim of connecting citizens with the people they have entrusted to take decisions on their behalf. The right to hold public bodies to account and to be able to see the principles of open, transparent government upheld is one which must continue to be protected.

Nonetheless, as the MOJ also notes, increased openness by public bodies must not to be reflected in the way information about individuals is used. Freedoms must not be compromised in the search for more convenient ways of working (which would include the growth in, often shared, databases). It thus states that it remains committed to seeking more efficient ways of working whilst ensuring effective mechanisms remain in place to protect liberty.

To ensure that rights are actively promoted, protected and upheld the MOJ states that it will among other things:

- ensure that the rights of individuals are balanced against the interests of the wider community;
- promote and publicise the HRA 1998 and its principles to government, public services and the wider public;
- equip public authorities to apply the Human Rights Act effectively through the provision of appropriate training and guidance;
- develop and deliver the Government's strategy for information sharing;
- establish a culture of freedom of information across the whole of the public sector, through advice, guidance and improved publication schemes.

OPENNESS AND TRANSPARENCY

By all the signs, the UK Government is thus committed to greater openness and transparency in public affairs; both objectives that serve as a reminder of the already changed face of public life given the levels of secrecy, confidentiality and lack of publicity that prevailed historically in relation to many aspects of public affairs in the UK. The MOJ, which took over lead responsibility in this regard from the DCA, is also committed to freedom of information. Further and more general moves in the direction of open government are evident from the introduction[21] to *The Governance of Britain*, where alongside extensive statements about the desirability of more inclusive and shared approaches to government and democracy the claim is made that constitutional changes already made since 1997 include, among other things, 'introducing the Freedom of Information Act, increasing transparency and the ability to hold the Government to account'. The MOJ/DCA has since 2005 published an *Information Rights Journal* for people working in the information rights field and which it describes as 'a reference tool capturing the latest developments in freedom of information, data protection and the Environmental Information Regulations ... an important resource which will grow with time [and] provide summaries of recent decisions which have emerged from the Information Commissioner's office [below]'.[22] But the most important thing would seem to be the general stance of Government and the MOJ and official thinking on how openness links to democracy as captured in *The Governance of Britain*:

> Freedom of information must not be a free-for-all ... Democracy underpins the fabric of our society. It is the embodiment of our values. It unites us and brings communities together, providing a voice for those in society who are vulnerable or marginalised. Democracy provides the right for all to have a say ... It is a right which it would be unthinkable to compromise. Yet it is a right we must do more to promote. Improving understanding of the democratic process, increasing access for those who wish to vote and engaging with those who would otherwise not vote are all things we must continue to strive for. Upholding democratic rights means we must maintain confidence in the integrity of our electoral process.

Freedom of information

The Freedom of Information Act 2000 was based on the White Paper, *Your Right to Know*.[23] It gives anyone the right to access information held by a public authority including central government departments such as the MOJ and Home Office. Anyone can make a request for information by writing or sending an email to the public authority concerned.

The term 'public authority' includes not just central government departments but also local authorities, local councils, general medical practitioners, hospitals, schools, colleges, police authorities, the armed forces and others.[24] Information that is made available can cover not just that concerning everyday public records, events or archive materials but that about such

---

[21] Reproduced within *Appendix VI* to this work.

[22] http://foi.gov.uk/reference/informationRightsJournal

[23] (1997); Cm 3818.

[24] This describes the situation in England and Wales and that is reflected in similar arrangements under the devolved Governments in Scotland and Northern Ireland.

sensitive matters as counter-terrorism and intelligence work where this is not counter to national security. However, all is not perfect and there have sometimes been criticisms concerning the non-availability of information relating to the workings of Parliament itself (while there have also been pre-MOJ moves to extend the extent to which correspondence and information might be exempted from disclosure) as well as the introduction of fees above a given volume of data. There have been hints that increased charges might be imposed more generally, which raises questions in relation to openness and accessibility; but it has been pointed out by Government that citizens should not be allowed to impose open-ended research burdens on the state.

Requests for information

In keeping with the objective of making information freely available, any person can make a request under the Act. There are no restrictions, e.g. on age, nationality, or where someone lives. The only formality required is a letter or email to the public authority in question stating that the person concerned believes that it holds information that he or she would like to see, together with that person's name, the address where he or she can be contacted and a description of the information that he or she wishes to see (in practice with as many useful identifying details as possible). There is no need for any reason or further explanation by the applicant.

Public authorities must comply with such requests promptly, and normally provide such information within 20 working days. If they need more time, they must write telling the correspondent and stating when they will be able to answer the request, and why more time is needed. This is also subject to certain exemptions in the 2000 Act that require public authorities to consider whether it is in the public interest to withhold the information. In some instances consideration of the public interest takes longer, when an estimate should be given about when a decision will have been reached.

The Information Commissioner

The Information Commissioner's Office (ICO) is an independent public body set up to promote access to official information and to protect personal information by promoting good practice, ruling on complaints, providing information to individuals and organizations, and taking appropriate action when the law is not complied with by public authorities. It is an independent public office, headed by an Information Commissioner that was established for the express purpose of encouraging on the one hand access to official information and on the other the protection of official information where this is appropriate. Among other things, the ICO enforces and oversees the Data Protection Act 1998, the 2000 Act itself and various environmental privacy and electronic communications regulations:

Our main functions are educating and influencing (we promote good practice and give information and advice), resolving problems (we resolve eligible complaints from people who think their rights have been breached) and enforcing (we use legal sanctions against those who ignore or refuse to accept their obligations).

In looking after citizen's rights and making sure that organizations comply with the law, the ICO also carries out associated research projects.

CHAPTER 7

Sentencing Policy
and Guidelines

CHAPTER 7

Sentencing Policy and Guidelines

The term 'sentencing policy' is often used in a fairly loose sense to describe the official line on crime and punishment and variously to mean the broad stance of the Government, courts, HM Prison Service (HMPS) and the National Probation Service (NPS) with regard to such matters: whether there should be a tough, harsh and uncompromising approach or regime, or a relatively liberal, tolerant, understanding and forward-looking one, e.g. via education, special programmes, drug treatment, managing offenders, improving social conditions or what is known as restorative justice.[1] Whichever side of this eternal divide opinion falls on, the term 'sentencing policy' is also used in two quite different senses, between which it is important to distinguish. The term may be used in:

- a *political* sense; or
- a *judicial* sense.

Parliamentary legislation and judicial discretion
In the first of these senses, the *political* one, sentencing policy results from decisions made by Parliament expressed in the form of legislation and its creation is part of the normal democratic process. Here, 'policy' signifies such matters as what jurisdiction and powers of punishment judges and magistrates (i.e. the judiciary) are to be given so that they, acting on behalf of the state and its citizens, can impose sentences on convicted offenders. Usually, this is by reference to a given maximum punishment, e.g. imprisonment related to a given type of offence, e.g. seven years imprisonment and/or a fine (as in the case of theft) or 14 years and/or a fine (as with burglary of a dwelling-house).[2] Parliament sets these parameters in Acts of Parliament and it is then for the members of the judiciary to pass sentence in individual cases depending on the precise facts and merits of each case, applying their judicial discretion (*Chapter 2*). In modern times, Parliament has also provided an overall statutory sentencing framework containing criteria and factors that judges must consider. Occasionally, mandatory (i.e. obligatory) sentences exist but this is relatively rare (see under *The Sentencing Framework*, below).

In the second sense above, the *judicial* one, sentencing policy connotes the broad levels of sentence that are deemed by judges and magistrates to be appropriate for given offences within the maximum powers granted by Parliament. Here the term

---

[1] A main aim of restorative justice is not punishment or retribution outright, but to repair the harm as between an offender and his or her victim and society.
[2] There is a lower ceiling for magistrates' courts: see *Appendix III*.

'sentencing policy' may be regarded as unacceptable, since 'policy' is seen by some judges and magistrates as connoting a fixed outcome – the very antithesis of the varying outcomes that result from using discretion. But there is little doubt that the word 'policy' is regularly encountered in this second context, as it also is on occasion to describe the more general stance of the judiciary towards, e.g. the use or not of imprisonment in general. Hence, judicial missives in this regard tend to be couched in cautious terms with warnings or caveats that any such policy represents no more than an initial guide or 'starting point'. The terms 'judicial guidance' or 'sentencing guidelines' are thus more generally and frequently used (below).

Promulgation of sentencing information
The Lord Chancellor has a statutory duty to publish information about sentencing. Section 175 Criminal Justice Act 2003 extended a key provision: that in section 95 Criminal Justice Act 1991, under which he or she is under a duty to publish information to people engaged in the administration of justice concerning the costs of different types of sentence and a range of discrimination issues extending to such matters as race, religion, gender or hate crime. Thus, various people concerned with the administration of justice now regularly receive information from the MOJ (formerly from the Home Office) so that they can be aware of 'the relative effectiveness of different sentences in … preventing re-offending and … promoting public confidence in the criminal justice system'.

THE SENTENCING FRAMEWORK

Maximum powers of punishment normally appear in the Act of Parliament creating an offence, e.g. the Theft Act 1968 that creates various offences (mainly of) dishonesty. In contrast, the wider sentencing framework and its component parts – setting out the powers of judges and magistrates – to impose different levels of sentence: discharges, fines, community sentences and imprisonment, etc. and related criteria – are usually contained in what are termed Criminal Justice Acts (CJAs).[3] Major CJAs tend to involve prior and wide-ranging consultation with interested parties and the Parliamentary timetables may be preceded by a Government White Paper or Green Paper. Depending on the extent of the prospective changes, consultation may also involve seminars, working groups or task forces in which representatives of the various stakeholder or partner services, including the courts, HM Prison Service (HMPS) and National Probation Service (NPS) take part. This serves to test the interaction of potential decisions by one part of the Criminal Justice System (CJS) with others. The government department with

---

[3] Often so-called 'Criminal Justice Acts' do not bear this title, as e.g. with the Crime and Disorder Act 1998 or Serious and Organized Crime and Police Act 2005 (containing a mix of police and court powers). Similarly, there is a Management of Offenders Bill.

lead responsibility for this was the Home Office and is now the MOJ. The former developed the first comprehensive statutory sentencing framework in the Criminal Justice Act 1991.[4] This was replaced by that now in place under the Criminal Justice Act 2003.[5] Managing sentence-related aspects of the law-making and law reform process is a key task for the MOJ (see also generally, *Chapter 5*). Guidance or guidelines created largely by members of the judiciary itself are then overlaid on this framework as an aid to decision-making by judges and magistrates when arriving at an appropriate level of punishment, e.g. custody or a community sentence for a particular offence and the amount of punishment – what is called 'restriction of liberty' – within that level (see *Sentencing Guidelines*, below).

Aspects of the sentencing framework

It would be impossible in a book of this type to describe the whole sentencing framework in all its complexity. What is important here, it seems, is to convey those things that in broad terms the sentencing framework sets out to achieve, highlight the scale of the related tasks facing the MOJ and its component parts, and to emphasise that whatever the Lord Chancellor or MOJ officials may do in this field they must approach the judicial function with sensitivity (*Chapter 2*). The framework in the Criminal Justice Act 2003 is contained principally in Part 12 of that Act and its associated provisions. Part 12 is extensive, comprising nine 'chapters' covering the general structure of the sentencing framework and specific aspects of it, ranging from life sentences and sentences for public protection (SPPs)[6] to long-term sentences of imprisonment (over four years) and short-term sentences of imprisonment (12 months to under four years) to what are termed 'sentences below 12 months'.[7] There is then a tier of community-based disposals - known as the generic community sentence[8] – from whose menu of 'requirements' a court may select those most suitable for a given offender in a particular case. These requirements concern:

---

[4] Based on the White Paper, *Crime Justice and Protecting the Public* (1990); Cm. 965.

[5] The provisions of the CJA 2003 are set out in some detail in *The Criminal Justice Act 2003: A Guide to the New Procedures and Sentencing* (2004), Gibson B, Waterside Press. The changes stem from the White Paper, *Justice For All* (2002); Cm, 5563, that was based on certain recommendations in *Making Punishments Work: Report of a Review of the Sentencing Framework for England and Wales* (2001); Home Office (also known as 'The Halliday report'). The Halliday report recommended, among other things, that the sentencing framework should do more to support crime reduction and reparation whilst at the same time meeting the needs of punishment. There is an Offender Management and Sentencing Bill in progress that would affect the framework.

[6] Sometimes called IPPs (imprisonment for public protection).

[7] Some of which still await implementation.

[8] Greater use of such requirements is one way to tackle prison overcrowding: *Chapter 3*.

- unpaid work to be carried out by the offender;
- his or her taking part in certain activities;
- similarly participation in programmes;
- a prohibition preventing him or her taking part in given activities;
- a curfew;
- exclusion from certain places;
- his or her place of residence;
- mental health treatment;
- drug rehabilitation;
- alcohol treatment;
- general supervision by a probation officer; and
- attendance at an attendance centre (up to age 25).

Electronic monitoring (known as 'tagging') can be added to any of the 12 basic requirements as the court deems appropriate and in relation to certain of these requirements it normally will be. The 2003 Act also deals with such matters as deferment of sentence (adjourning it to see how the offender continues to conduct himself or herself in his or her day-to-day life before imposing sentence), and drug treatment and testing. It also makes special provisions with regard, e.g. to firearms offences. There are extensive provisions about release from custody on parole, release licences and post-custody supervision; and relating to breach, enforcement and recall to prison (see, generally, *Chapter 3* of this work).

At the time of the 2003 Act, its new framework was promoted as being clearer and more flexible than in the 1991 Act. A further intention of Government was that courts would be equipped to provide every offender with a sentence 'that best meets the needs of his or her particular case', it being claimed that this way he or she would be more effectively managed. The new arrangements occurred at the same time as the fundamental reconstruction of HM Prison Service (HMPS) and the National Probation Service (NPS) to create the National Offender Management Service (NOMS) as described in *Chapter 3*.

In a further and directly judicially related context, section 174 of the 2003 Act contains a general duty - other than where a sentence is mandatory, fixed or otherwise required by law (below) - for a court to give reasons for and to explain the effect of that sentence in 'ordinary language and in general terms', and in particular for departing from any SGC guidelines. The provision also sets out other, special situations where an explanation is required.

Mandatory sentences: a note

Historically, the only mandatory sentence was the death penalty for murder, now replaced by a mandatory life sentence. In modern times, Parliament has passed various measures that have the effect of curtailing the discretion of the judiciary in relation to specific areas of sentencing: these include additional mandatory sentences of imprisonment such as those under the 'three strikes' law,[9] indefinite sentences for public protection from what, in effect, are dangerous, violent or sexual offenders, and minimum sentences for certain firearms offences. The dangerous offender provisions are mainly addressed to three distinct categories of offenders:

- people sentenced to life imprisonment (often called 'lifers');
- certain other long-term prisoners who receive SPPs (above); and
- other, possibly lesser - though still dangerous violent and sexual - offenders for whom the Act creates extended sentences.

The extended part of such a sentence involves supervision in the community on release (often for a substantial period as set by the court), once an 'appropriate custodial term' – known as a tariff and fixed by the judge – commensurate with the seriousness of the offence – has been served. Such sentences may attract complaints from the judiciary that their hands are being increasingly tied, making true justice, fairness and consistency difficult or impossible. However, the doctrine of the supremacy of Parliament dictates that, ultimately, this is a matter for elected representatives, albeit that this is the kind of topic where events can be driven by untutored media pressure; there normally being little news value in mitigation or explanations put forward by offenders. Situations in which judges have been obliged to pass certain sentences of this kind have led to tensions between the Government, Parliament and the judiciary and any future new constitution might be expected to touch on such issues. A similar situation developed in relation to mandatory tariffs for offenders subject to life imprisonment or SPPs where, certainly at one stage and with a degree of irony, the Government sought to blame the judiciary for the escalating prison population (*Chapter 3*) – a slight later withdrawn. More generally, the convention is that ministers do not publicly criticise the judiciary in this way but rather have respect for its role.

The wide-ranging extent of sentencing considerations
As already intimated above, a wide range of inter-connected matters affect sentencing decisions. One practice that has developed is that of structured decision-making, which seeks to ensure that all relevant matters are taken into account and that irrelevant matters are discounted. This method involves the court in working through a series of stages or steps and also formulating

---

[9] As it is known in the USA. Strictly speaking in the UK it is normally (but not always) a two-strikes law, i.e. imprisonment is mandatory for a certain specified offence.

reasons as it does so. Among key aspects of the framework that can only be mentioned here in barest outline[10] are such matters as:

- threshold tests for:
  - — community sentences (known as the 'serious enough' test, i.e. serious enough for a community sentence rather than a fine or discharge); and
  - — custodial sentences (known as the 'so serious' test, i.e. where the offence is so serious that neither a discharge, fine or community sentence can be justified for the particular offence in question);
- statutory purposes of sentencing (see further below); and
- an emphasis on:
  - — drug-testing and rehabilitation, both before and as part of a sentence;
  - — electronic monitoring in relation to a community order or when an offender is released from prison after or during a custodial sentence including on what is known as home detention curfew (HDC);
  - — discounts (in effect) for a timely plea of guilty;[11]
  - — the idea of reviewable sentences and far stricter enforcement;
  - — totality and proportionality, i.e. if several sentences are being imposed on someone at the same time this should be looked at globally or 'in the round' and more generally all (non-mandatory) sentences should be in proportion (or at least not disproportionate) to the seriousness of the offence or offences committed by the offender;
  - — disqualifications, especially those concerning working with children;
  - — new approaches to the imposition and collection of financial penalties;
  - — priority being given to compensation;[12] and
  - — identifying and dealing appropriately with mental impairment.

Statutory purposes of sentencing and associated provisions
The CJA 2003 introduced statutory purposes of sentencing that 'any court dealing with an offender . . . must have regard to' in arriving at its decision. These are listed in section 142(1) CJA 2003 as follows:

(a) the punishment of offenders;
(b) the reduction of crime (including through deterrence);
(c) the reform and rehabilitation of offenders;
(d) protecting the public; and
(e) reparation by offenders to people affected by their offences.

Section 143 CJA 2003 also sets out certain matters a sentencer *must* consider in determining the seriousness of an offence:

---

[10] The framework is set out in *A Guide to the CJA 2003, etc.* noted in an earlier footnote.
[11] All now the subject of work and guidance by the SGC.
[12] See, also, now the reference to the Victim Surcharge Fund in *Chapter 8.*

- the offender's *culpability* in committing the offence; and
- any *harm* caused by the offence, intended by it, or which 'might foreseeably' have been caused.

There are some situations in which a court is required by law to treat an offence as more serious than it would otherwise have done, e.g. if it is committed whilst on bail, involves racial or religious aggravation (also known as 'hate crime') or there are previous relevant convictions and thus, in practice (and other things being equal), the court should use a more severe penalty. Other categories have been added to this rule concerning hostility based on sexual orientation or disability (also sometimes called hate crimes) and offences linked to terrorism.

SENTENCING GUIDELINES

Sentencing guidelines have a long and reputable history. Hence, e.g. Court of Appeal guidelines stemming from certain key rulings by that court when dealing with an appeal against a sentence of the Crown Court have long been termed 'guideline rulings' or 'guideline cases' and attracted respect across the court and legal system. Analogous apparatus have included guidelines created by the Magistrates' Association for use by its members and other practitioners in the magistrates' courts. These processes are being largely superseded by the work of the Sentencing Guidelines Council (SGC). Neither the home secretary in the past nor the Lord Chancellor today has any final or definitive say in such matters even though he or she is the responsible minister vis-à-vis sentencing policy in the broad *political* sense outlined at the start of this chapter. It is the Lord Chief Justice who - as head of the judiciary post the Constitutional Reform Act 2005 – leads the SGC. It is the SGC that now promulgates the main advice on such matters and that thus guides the discretion of all judges and magistrates. The Lord Chancellor has certain associated rights and formal channels via which he or she may seek to influence the SGC. This can include providing research (see, generally, *Chapter 8*), information and proposals to the extent that such approaches remain legitimate.

Sentencers also rely on reported judgements from a myriad of individual appeal outcomes in cases that have reached the Court of Appeal, together with (infrequent) *Practice Directions*. In future, the SGC will be the ultimate authority in terms of sentencing guidelines and once these reach the stage where they are no longer draft guidelines but are 'definitive', courts must have regard to them and give their reasons for any departure from them (section 172 CJA 2003).

The Sentencing Guidelines Council (SGC)

The SGC was a key development of the CJA 2003 (see section 167). It consists of the Lord Chief Justice (who is designated as its chair by the statute), seven judicial members and four non-judicial members. The provisions set out the basis upon which both kinds of member are eligible for appointment and are to be appointed. Whereas judicial members are to be selected from the various ranks of the judiciary so as to reflect the views of people regularly dealing with criminal cases, non-judicial individuals are only eligible for appointment if they appear to have experience in one or more of the following areas: policing; criminal prosecution; criminal defence; or the promotion of the welfare of victims of crime. People 'eligible by virtue of experience' include the Director of Public Prosecutions (DPP). Non-judicial appointees must include at least one person appearing to have experience in each of the areas mentioned above. The Lord Chancellor can also appoint an observer with experience of sentencing policy and administration of sentences and he or she may attend and speak at meetings.

The Lord Chief Justice must appoint a deputy chair from the judicial members and can nominate an eligible judicial 'substitute' to attend when he or she is absent. The SGC must make an annual report to ministers on the exercise of its functions. The SGC is supported by a permanent secretariat that also acts as a liaison point for other interested parties and that, e.g. administers ongoing consultations. The interaction of the SGC and SAP, below, can be seen in a range of published guidelines, advice or proposals on matters such as assault, Bail Act 1976 offences, domestic violence, robbery, sexual offences, manslaughter and causing death by dangerous driving as well as referring certain matters such as child pornography to the Court of Appeal.[13]

The Sentencing Advisory Panel (SAP)

The SGC is supported by a Sentencing Advisory Panel (SAP) (originally set up under the Crime and Disorder Act 1998 and thus pre-dating the SGC by some five years). The SAP is no longer confined, as it once was, to suggesting 'approaches' to particular types of offences. It is appointed by the Lord Chancellor (after consultation with the Lord Chief Justice) who also appoints its chair. It is responsible for research into sentencing and for producing reports and information. Outcomes of its deliberations are communicated to the SCG for consideration alongside other information, data and relevant materials. This may also be by way of a proposal to the SGC pursuant to section 171 CJA 2003, which the SGC is then duty bound to consider. Conversely, the SGC must notify the SAP about any other proposed or revised guidelines and as part of that process the SAP must also in turn (and except in cases of urgency) consult with people stipulated by the SGC and, in effect, respond to the SGC.

---

[13] Full details appear at www.sentencing-guidelines.gov.uk

Guidelines

A key aspect of the provisions are those whereby the SGC may from time to time consider whether to frame sentencing guidelines and under which the Lord Chancellor[14] may propose to the SGC that this occur (or that existing guidelines should be revised) in respect of:

- offences or offenders of a particular category; or
- a particular matter affecting sentencing.

The SGC must then consider such proposals (plus any from the SAP) and, in effect, decide whether or not to act upon them. This discretion represents a critical buffer in terms of the independence of the judiciary. There are the following statutory criteria when considering the issue of sentencing guidelines:

- the need to promote consistency in sentencing;
- the sentences imposed by courts in England and Wales;
- the cost of different sentences and their relative effectiveness in preventing offending;
- the need to promote public confidence in the criminal justice system; and
- the views communicated to the SGC by the SAP.

The SGC can act of its own initiative to create guidelines and there are various provisions aimed at keeping SGC guidelines current and up-to-date. As intimated above, the SGC must consider whether to frame guidelines if it receives a guidelines proposal from the SAP (as it must where this stems from the Lord Chancellor: above). Guidelines must be kept under review and the SGC must revise them if appropriate (section 170(5)); there is a statutory process of drafts, consultation and eventual publication (section 170(8), (9)). As already indicated above, courts will have to follow the definitive guidelines of the SGC or explain themselves alongside the new statutory reasoning process already referred to earlier in this chapter.

Since its inception, the SGC has produced various guidelines, including those addressed towards reduction of a sentence following a plea of guilty; and what it terms 'advice' on sentencing for assault and Bail Act offences.

---

[14] Post-MOJ. Formerly this fell to the home secretary, quite correctly in terms of the then legislative function concerning criminal offences, but somewhat questionably in overall constitutional terms. The pre-2003 Act proposals included one suggestion that Parliament should have a role in the framing of sentencing guidelines or that a (then) home office official should sit as a member of the SGC. Again, an entrenched constitution (*Chapter 6*) might be expected to cover such matters.

CHAPTER 8

Miscellaneous Responsibilities of the MOJ

CHAPTER 8

Miscellaneous Responsibilities of the MOJ

The Ministry of Justice (MOJ) has an extensive range of duties and responsibilities that are not dealt with elsewhere in this book. They range across the entire constitutional and justice framework, including such key matters as making sure that adequate procedures or codes of practice exist in relation to all its functions, not least those relating to the everyday operation of criminal, civil and family courts. As part of this wide remit, the MOJ sponsors a range of organizations or bodies, such as advisory boards and other sponsored organizations of the kind listed in *Appendix II* to this work. These range from the Advisory Committee on the General Commissioners of Income Tax, to the Correctional Services Accreditation Panel (*Chapter 3*), to the Advisory Council on Tribunals (*Chapter 2*). At the end of this chapter, under the heading *Some Other Key Areas of Responsibility*, a selection from the MOJ's diverse range of responsibilities, noted in snapshot form, serves to give some indication of the sheer scale of the MOJ's wider preoccupations.

VICTIMS AND WITNESSES

Without satisfactory arrangements to encourage victims of crime to come forward and for witnesses, whether victims or not, to give information to the police and if need be testimony from the witness box in a courtroom, the Criminal Justice System (CJS) would soon become unworkable. Historically, neither had what might be described as 'a fair deal' and there are even today concerns about the way that some of them are relegated to the sidelines or treated as mere adjuncts to a story that is all about a suspect, accused person or offender. In continuing with existing initiatives to 'look after' victims and witnesses, and to ensure that the people whom the system is there to serve are 'at the heart of the justice system', the MOJ is committed to what, Lord Falconer, the then Lord Chancellor, described not only as 'a practical need [but] also a social and moral imperative':

> People who use the justice system are often at times of great difficulty in their lives; as a victim or witness in a criminal case, or those going through family or civil justice, or the coroners courts. The experience of justice can be traumatic, harrowing and intimidating. We must ensure that people feel confident to come forward, and that they will be given the necessary support to do so – before, during and after they have gone through the system ... No one can undo the harm done through being a victim of crime, or obviate the loss felt by the bereaved going through the coroners' system,

or remove the damage that can be done to families going through child care proceedings. But the system can work better to lessen the distress … We will do this through a combination of making emotional and practical support more accessible, and by improving processes to better suit their needs. We are currently looking at how we can provide that practical and emotional support for families of murder and manslaughter victims.[1]

Hence there are corresponding moves both in the courts and across justice-related processes to provide improved liaison, information and updates concerning the progress of a case and what is to happen at a given stage. Among other things, the MOJ has stated that it is committed to speeding up the delivery of justice so that the time taken, and the number of appearances in court that a victim or witness may be faced with, are significantly reduced. It has issued both a *Code of Practice for Victims of Crime*[2] and a *Witness Charter* which are designed to establish and improve upon common standards of care. In addition, a new Public Protection Advocacy Scheme is being introduced in relation to oral hearings for prisoners seeking to be released by the Parole Board. This allows the victim to state to the board, through an advocate, what the impact of releasing an offender might be on them, e.g. if the offender returned to his or her original haunts or to close or overbearing proximity to the victim or his or her family. Similarly, within the community, the MOJ is working with a range of organizations to ensure that emotional and practical support is available from trusted sources, to help guide people through what are often difficult and distressing times.

The Victim Surcharge Fund

Immediately following the announcement of the MOJ in May 2007, it was also announced that an extra £5.6 million[3] was being made available to develop improved services for victims of crime. This money came from the proceeds of a Victim Surcharge Fund established earlier in 2007 under which £15 from every court fine goes towards that fund. According to the MOJ justice minister, David Hanson MP, the plan is also to 'develop and roll out improved services for victims of crime'.[4] He also stated that improved services included telephoning victims of crime within 48 hours of a police referral to Victim Support (below):

> At present most victims are contacted by letter … Tailored emotional support for victims of crime that better meets their individual needs such as access to counselling

---

[1] Lord Falconer has since become patron of the North of England Victims Association (NEVA), many of whose members have suffered in this way.

[2] The original *Victims Charter* was issued in 1990 and replaced by a *Victims' Code of Practice* in 2005.

[3] According to the Government's own figures it has nearly trebled the amount of money for Victim Support from £11.2 million in 1997 to £30 million in 2007.

[4] Speaking at a Victims Support National Conference at Warwick University.

and buying in specialist services for particular offences like domestic violence and road deaths ... Immediate help like organizing lock fitting, alarm repairing and transport, such as taxis, where these are not available through other organizations

At the same time, the 'heartbreaking' and 'life changing' effects of being a victim of crime when 'no-one can stop the hurt' were acknowledged, leaving the state to try and reduce the impact that crime has on such victims:

> One way we have done that is to ask victims of crime what help and support they want, test that it works properly and then provide the money and infrastructure to make it happen nationally ... Crucially the Government is working in close partnership with Victim Support so that the benefits are swift and effective. Victims of crime expect and deserve to be put at the heart of the criminal justice system and the extra funding for improved services aims to do that ... The improved services for victims were piloted for six months in Salford, Nottingham and North Yorkshire after the Government provided £1 million. Evaluation has shown that they were successful, they will now be rolled out across England and Wales from September.

Other enhanced services for victims include: counselling, window locks, glazing repair, security lights, personal alarms, panic alarms, security information and advice, financial assistance and distribution of advice about the Criminal Injuries Compensation Authority (CICA) now also sponsored by the MOJ, below.

The Criminal Injuries Compensation Authority (CICA)

The CICA administers the criminal injuries compensation scheme throughout England, Scotland and Wales. It pays compensation to people who have been the victims of violent crimes. The scheme operates from Glasgow and London. Since 1964 when the first scheme was established, CICA (and the former Criminal Injuries Compensation Board which it replaced) has paid out some £3 billion in compensation.

The aim is to provide victims with some material recognition of their pain and suffering and to allow society to express its regret to them. For most of CICA's history, awards were set according to what the victim would have received in a successful civil claim against the offender. Since 1996, the level of compensation is determined according to a tariff, set by Parliament. The scheme was revised in 2001 and the tariff includes descriptions of over 400 different kinds of injuries that can result from an offence against the victim. Tariff amounts range across 25 levels starting at £1,000 and rising to £250,000.

In certain situations, when applicants have also suffered financial loss, e.g. through loss of earnings or earning capacity, the cost of medical or other care, or because they were dependent on someone who was murdered, they may apply for additional compensation.

Around 450 staff from both the MOJ and Scottish Executive are employed by CICA to decide upon applications: some 65,000 applications per year. Almost £200 million a year is disbursed to victims at current rates.

Victim impact statements (VIPs)

This notion of crime and its impact on a victim has also been formalised within court processes with the introduction of what are known as 'victim impact statements' (VIPs). These are usually drawn up by a probation officer and attached to his or her pre-sentence report (PSR). They cannot affect sentence in the full sense that they become a reason for increasing or decreasing a sentence but they may, potentially, have an overall effect both in relation to the components of a sentence, its administration and ultimately, issues affecting a prisoner's release date. The National Probation Service (NPS) has worked closely (as did its forerunner local probation services) with victims since the late-1980s and according to the MOJ is committed to more contact and involvement with the victims of serious sexual and violent crime in particular. Recognition of the benefits of such victim-related work led to provisions requiring certain official contact with victims in the Criminal Justice and Court Services Act 2000. When they request it, victims are nowadays kept informed of an offender's release arrangements and in some cases it becomes imperative that the victim's situation is included in the determination of the offender's post-release supervision plan.

Victim Support (VS)[5]

Victim Support is an independent charity that helps victims of crime to cope with the effects of crime. It provides free and confidential support and information to assist a victim in dealing with his or her experience. VS also works to promote and advance the rights of victims and witnesses generally. It operates through local VS branches that lend support also to their families and friends, including by the provision of information. VS also runs the Witness Service (below). It has a helpline, called Victim Supportline.[6] VS is operated by volunteers and supported via donations and the proceeds of VS's online appeals and ventures.

Witnesses

As already intimated, witnesses often suffer from the same sense of alienation that victims do when they come into contact with regular participants in the justice process who naturally tend to feel 'at home' in what for a witness are strange surroundings – though the needs of witnesses may be quite different or

---

[5] As the laws and systems affecting victims and witnesses differ across the UK and Ireland, there are now separate Victim Support websites for England and Wales, Scotland, Northern Ireland and the Republic of Ireland.

[6] 0845 30 30 900. See also generally, www.victimsupport.org.uk

more specialised than those of victims of crime. Hence the creation of a separate body of volunteers known as the Witness Service. At the furthest extreme, sophisticated arrangements exist, via the Home Office, the police (and where applicable HM Prison Service) for the protection of witnesses who are vulnerable to physical abuse or intimidation. This extends to the use of separate prison accommodation for prisoners on Rule 43 as it is known, safe houses and the provision of witness protection by way of a bodyguard where this is necessary.

STATISTICS, RESEARCH AND CONSULTATION

The MOJ publishes a range of statistics relating to the operation of the criminal and civil justice systems including on various aspects of criminal justice policy, crime, sentencing and family justice policy, as well as those relating to its other areas of responsibility. As noted in *Chapter 7*, statistics are also provided to the Sentencing Guidelines Council (SGC), whether in conjunction with the work of the Sentencing Advisory Panel (SAP) or the MOJ's own proposals for guidance and advice to judges and magistrates. Certain statistics (marked NS in the list below) are designated as 'national statistics' and are produced in accordance with a national statistics code of practice, itself currently under review as a result of the Green Paper, *The Governance of Britain*.[7] By way of example, the MOJ 2007/2008 statistical publication programme includes figures in relation to:

- arrests for offences which are classed as notifiable to the police and the operation of certain police powers under the Police and Criminal Evidence Act 1984 (PACE) (NS);
- average times from arrest to sentence for persistent young offenders (NS);
- company winding up and bankruptcy petition statistics (NS);
- deaths reported by coroners (NS);
- the *Criminal Statistics Annual Report* (NS);
- the Freedom of Information Act 2000;
- mortgage and landlord possession (NS);
- motoring offences and breath tests (NS);
- the prison population (monthly) (see, generally, *Chapter 3*);
- prison population projections (NS);
- prison and probation statistics (annual) (NS);
- probation (quarterly);
- race and the criminal justice system;
- re-offending by adults (NS);
- re-offending by juveniles (NS);

---

[7] (2007) Cm 7170: see in particular *Chapter 6*.

- sentencing (by way of a sentencing brief) (quarterly);
- sentencing (annual statistics) (NS);
- time intervals for criminal proceedings in magistrates' courts;[8]
- judicial statistics; and
- criminal and civil business of the courts in England and Wales.

Research

An MOJ research programme involving research by MOJ staff or outside bodies such as university departments, or the voluntary sector, underpins all its responsibilities, leading to a range of publications, information and statistics, including specially commissioned projects where appropriate. There were reports in 2007 on 'Restorative Justice: The Views of Victims and Offenders'; and the 'Third Report from the Evaluation of Three Schemes: Diversity and Fairness in the Jury System'. The latter report examines whether the juror summoning process discriminates against black and minority ethnic (BME) groups, whether jurors serving at Crown Courts are representative of the local population in terms of ethnicity, age, gender, employment, income and religion, and whether a defendant's ethnicity affects the decision-making of racially-mixed juries. Another example is 'Go-Between', an evaluation of intermediary pathfinder projects for supporting witnesses and helping to bring cases to court in six areas of England and Wales.

One criticism of government-sponsored research has been that it always had to be done on the government's own terms and conditions, and in pursuit of its own political objectives. Concern has therefore been expressed about its independence, and sometimes about the way in which government has tried to control the results. Different concerns arise over developments in the physical sciences, where the issues are more likely to relate to the legitimacy and accountability of the uses to which research or statistics are put.

Overall government responsibility for statistics and research on criminal justice is located within the Research, Development and Statistics Directorate (RDSD) which is an integral part of the Home Office. The RDSD also serves the MOJ and other government departments. Its web-site[9] states:

> We provide information that helps ministers and policy-makers to take evidence-based decisions and also help the police, probation service, the courts and immigration officials to do their job as effectively as possible. We do so both by maintaining the various statistical services published by the Home Office [and presumably, now, in relevant areas, of its responsibilities the MOJ] and by carrying out research ourselves or commissioning others to do so.

---

[8] See also *Chapter 1* for some statistics concerning the MOJ itself.

[9] www.homeoffice.gov.uk/rds

Far more might be added in a different kind of book about the influence and perceived shortcomings of government-based research amongst, e.g. criminologists and similar experts. Presumably, it was a similar and underlying sense of unease that caused questions to be raised in *The Governance of Britain* concerning the nature, use and oversight of official statistics.[10]

Consultation

Quite apart from its own standing advisory arrangements, the extent of which can be judged from *Appendix II* to this work, the MOJ regularly engages in wider consultation exercises, conferences and debates and puts out consultation papers containing proposals for change and ideas for new policies right across its many areas of responsibility. These are published to seek the views of partner departments and agencies, experts and members of the general public so as to allow the opportunity for wide-ranging comment. Anyone can respond to such consultation papers within whatever timetable exists in relation to a particular consultation excercise. Long overdue, this process might perhaps be expected to become more inclusive and open in the context of the MOJ's declared stance towards public affairs and the rights of citizens as indicated by post-MOJ pronouncements and its flagship consultation paper, *The Governance of Britain.*

SOME OTHER KEY AREAS OF RESPONSIBILITY

As noted at the start of this chapter, it is not possible to cover every further aspect of MOJ responsibility in a book of this kind. The following snapshots are representative of the wide range of services and advisory functions provided, overseen, sponsored or otherwise pursued by the MOJ.[11]

Alternative dispute resolution (ADR)

MOJ strategies involve moves to treat the courts as a last resort for people involved in civil or family disputes. Where possible, mediation is seen as an alternative to initiating court proceedings and it can be cheaper, speedier and less stressful. ADR is a voluntary process in which a neutral third party seeks to help the contending parties to come to an agreement concerning the best outcome of a dispute. Generally speaking for claims above £5,000, the MOJ helps to fund a National Mediation Helpline which can arrange a fixed-fee, time-limited mediation appointment with an accredited provider. For small claims, the MOJ offers an in-house court-based mediation service at no additional cost for people already involved in making or defending a claim. A Family Mediation

---

[10]   See also comments in *Crime, State and Citizen* (Second edition), pp. 138-141.

[11]   A good deal of information and web-links appear at www.justice.gov.uk/whatwedo

Helpline offers referrals to family mediation services. Legal aid may be available subject to eligibility. Such work is also underpinned by the voluntary sector organization, Mediation UK, and by a large number of private sector mediators. Some examples of the use of mediation appear within the following headings.

Burial and cremation

Burial grounds, memorials and the burial and exhumation of human remains are regulated by legislation in the interests of public health, decency and respect. These provisions are currently under review by the MOJ to ensure that they meet the needs of the 21st century. The MOJ decides upon applications for exhumation licences, regulates the removal of human remains from disused burial grounds and consider applications for the closure of churchyards. It also provides advice on burial law and practice for the public and for burial professionals, but is not responsible for the enforcement of such legislation. It is responsible for the law and policy on cremation, e.g. via the appointment of crematorium medical referees and the provision of guidance to doctors and other professionals who complete the various statutory forms that enable cremation to take place. The main legislation is the Cremation Act 1902, the Cremation Regulations 1930 and regulations made under the 1902 Act.

Claims management

Claims management regulation seeks to safeguard consumers by improving the operating standards of those who provide services relating to claims for compensation. Service providers must be authorised by a regulator or otherwise exempt. The Compensation Act 2006 provides the statutory framework for the prosecution of people who act without that authority. The MOJ is responsible for the regulation of claims management services, including via the authorisation of people who provide such services and monitors them to ensure compliance with relevant rules and regulations. It also provides information and guidance to claims management service providers, consumers, lawyers and the public on various aspects of this work.

Coroners

The MOJ is responsible for the law and policy relating to coroners. Coroners are independent judicial officers who are responsible for investigating violent, unnatural deaths or sudden deaths from unknown causes, including, e.g. deaths in police or prison custody. This involves inter-departmental liaison on such matters as dealing with queries, preparing advice or guidance to ministers, coroners, local authorities and the public – as well as liaison with coroners and bereavement groups, training for coroners and their staff; and supervision of the amalgamation of coroner districts. A programme of reform was established in

2003 and a draft Bill produced in 2006 that seeks to modernise the coroner service by creating a sound national framework and leadership, whilst ensuring that that service remains locally-based.

Devolved government and Crown dependencies

As part of its constitutional responsibilities, the MOJ is responsible for a range of matters concerning links to the devolved governments or assemblies of Scotland, Wales and Northern Ireland (matters that also fall for general discussion within the remit of the Green Paper, *The Governance of Britain*),[12] including by tendering advice to Government and its departments concerning devolution settlements.

The Crown dependencies are Jersey, Guernsey and the Isle of Man. They are not part of the UK and have their own elected assemblies, administrative, fiscal and legal systems and courts of law. They are not represented in the UK Parliament and UK legislation does not extend to them. The MOJ provides a channel of communication between the UK and the dependencies; and processes their legislation so that it can receive Royal assent; as well as consulting with the islands on extending UK legislation to them. The Lord Chancellor is responsible for recommending Crown appointments in each of the three islands.

Family matters, the breakdown of relationships and domestic violence

The MOJ is responsible for family justice, while the Department for Children, Schools and Families (DCSF) has responsibility for children, young people and families. Both departments now work together and with a range of other partners to deliver these policies. Quite apart from the administration of the Family Court System (FCS) (*Chapter 2*), the MOJ is responsible for the law on divorce, dissolution of civil partnership, annulment of marriage or civil partnership, and matters touching on the division of income and capital following separation (as to which it also encourages the use of mediation services to resolve any disputes: above). MOJ policies seek to ensure that when people divorce, or dissolve or annul a marriage or civil partnership, they are given help to do, e.g. in terms of seeking to reduce distress, especially to any children who may be involved.

The MOJ is also responsible for administering the law in England and Wales in relation to marriages and civil partnership, including related ceremonies and as to whether marriages or partnerships celebrated abroad are valid in England and Wales. It provides information to cohabitants on their legal rights; is funding a Law Commission report on the legal rights of cohabitants for when their relationship ends; and compiling a list of countries whose civil partnerships are accepted as valid in England and Wales. The MOJ has proposed considering

---

[12] Cm 7170.

'whether there should be specific laws to secure homes and finances for couples who cohabit'. More generally, in relation to 'relationship breakdown', the MOJ notes that

> parental separation is more common today than in the past. When contact disputes are handled badly, children can suffer. We are developing measures to improve information and advice to parents, promote alternative ways to resolve disputes, such as in-court conciliation, and mediation [above]. We also aim to give the courts more flexible powers in contact cases through the Children and Adoption Act 2006.

A sometimes closely-connected matter is domestic violence. In the everyday sense, this is a matter for the police and Crown prosecutors and various initiatives now exist to ensure the prosecution of perpetrators and the safety of victims, including via the provision of refuges, often by the voluntary sector. The MOJ defines domestic violence as 'any incident of threatening behaviour, violence or abuse (psychological, physical, sexual, financial or emotional) between adults who are or have been intimate partners or family members, regardless of gender or sexuality.' and is conscious that such violence may often be witnessed by children which, in turn, is a child protection issue. As part of its crime prevention and crime reduction aims, MOJ policy is 'to increase the rate [at which] domestic violence is reported and offenders brought to justice and to make sure that victims ... are adequately protected and supported'.

Electoral administration and modernisation

As part of its constitutional and democratic functions and again something that touches on *The Governance of Britain*, the MOJ's electoral administration responsibilities cover such matters as the reform of electoral legislation 'aimed at improving access, engagement, confidence in the system, extending openness and transparency; and maintaining professional delivery of elections and registration procedures', including by the implementation of changes contained in the Electoral Administration Act 2006. Its responsibilities cover UK-wide elections and (where applicable) referendums[13] and local government elections in England and Wales and the registration and enfranchisement of electors. Among other things, it sponsors the Independent Parliamentary Boundary Commissions (IPBC) for England and Wales.

According to the MOJ, electoral modernisation involves 'giving people choice in the way they exercise their vote' by developing policies and processes to make elections more accessible, improving participation, enhancing security and improving their efficiency and cost-effectiveness. In this, it works alongside various organizations, including the Electoral Commission, administrators and

---

[13] Except that mayoral referendums in Wales are devolved to the Welsh Assembly.

suppliers of initiatives such as pilot schemes to test innovations in local elections, and the Co-ordinated Online Record of Electors information system (CORE), which will in due course provide a single source of electoral registration information to authorised users of that data.

European and international obligations

The MOJ asserts that it works alongside other government departments and stakeholders to promote:

> the interests of the UK Government in the EU, the Council of Europe and other international forums, in matters of criminal, civil and family justice; data protection; human rights; and democratic engagement. We support the UK's legal services sector abroad and promote fair and effective justice systems internationally. We promote practical cooperation benefiting citizens, improving access to justice and rights, and liberalising markets.

As noted in *Chapter 6*, the MOJ plays a central role in relation to human rights.

Gender recognition

The Gender Recognition Act 2004 allows transsexual people to alter their legal gender and thus gain the rights and responsibilities of their new, 'acquired gender'. These rights include those to obtain a fresh birth certificate (where the birth was originally registered in the UK) and to marry in the acquired gender. The MOJ advises on policy concerning the 2004 Act. A Gender Recognition Panel (part of the Tribunals Service: *Chapter 2*) decides on applications to change gender and the issuing gender recognition certificates as well as keeping details of individuals who have been through this process strictly confidential.

Mental capacity

According to the MOJ, its mental capacity policies are 'about empowering and protecting people who may not be able to make decisions for themselves', as to which the Mental Capacity Act 2005 provides a statutory framework.[14] The MOJ is responsible, alongside the Department of Health, Welsh Assembly and Public Guardianship Office for implementing the 2005 Act. It is also responsible for providing information and guidance to individuals and their families, social and healthcare professionals and legal practitioners on aspects of this policy.

---

[14] Subject to any further impending legislation.

Royal and hereditary matters

Responsibility for royal matters originates with the ancient office of the King's Secretary. This was the channel of approach to the king for those subjects who had no direct right of access to the sovereign. Despite the historical transformation of the role, many of these original duties continue to fall to the Lord Chancellor. Hence, as the MOJ now asserts:

> We provide advice and expertise on the Royal prerogative; the use of the title 'Royal' and royal names, arms and emblems. We also manage the budget for lord-lieutenants' expenses, and administer the appointment process for deputy lieutenants.[15]

Women and criminal justice

The MOJ asserts that 'The Government is concerned about the increase in the female prison population over recent years and recognises the need to deliver a distinct response to women's offending'. A Women's Offending Reduction Programme (WORP) was launched in 2004 and focuses on improving community-based services providing interventions that are 'better tailored' to women and supporting greater use of community sentences (*Chapter 7*) as opposed to short prison sentences in particular. In 2007, Baroness Corston published her (then) Home Office-linked report, *Review of Women with Particular Vulnerabilities in the Criminal Justice System*.[16] The MOJ Women's Policy Team now leads coordination of a cross-government's response to that report.

Youth justice

Children and young people who break the law – often called juveniles or youths - are dealt with under a different arrangements to those for adults, including by youth courts and in many instances (and normally when the juvenile is making his or her first appearance at court) via what is known as a referral order, i.e. to an independent referral order panel that will wherever possible devise a plan for the juvenile in conjunction with a multi-agency youth offending team (YOT). One aim is to keep juveniles out of the criminal justice system whenever this is appropriate. Where a sentence proper is needed, there is a separate youth court sentencing framework.

As explained in *Chapter 1*, there are now shared arrangements for youth justice as between the MOJ and Department for Children, Schools and Families,

---

[15] Who act as the sovereign's representative in various parts of the country on formal occasions, e.g. to present awards, or who accompany the sovereign and other members of the Royal family during their visits to their area.

[16] (2007) Home Office. The report was issued before the Home Office split. The MOJ-led response to that report is scheduled for publication in 2007.

whilst the MOJ retains formal responsibility for the Youth Justice Board which oversees the youth justice system in England and Wales. With its partners, the MOJ thus works, as it does in relation to adults, to prevent offending and re-offending by children (10-13 inclusive) and young people (14-17) and if custodial sentences or other forms of restraint are needed, 'to ensure that custody for them is safe, secure and addresses the causes of their offending behaviour'.

The Secretary of State for Justice and Lord Chancellor

CHAPTER 9

The Secretary of State for Justice and Lord Chancellor

The Lord Chancellor has always been one of the most powerful of government ministers. A Cabinet minister selected by the prime minister, he or she formerly and until 2005 had the responsibility of appointing judges and magistrates, or in the case of the higher judiciary tendering advice to the prime minister to that end. Once appointed, judges could not – and still under the new arrangements described in *Chapter 2* - cannot simply be removed from office on a political whim, no matter how unpalatable to the executive their rulings might be, e.g. concerning the rights of citizens as against the state. Yet the Lord Chancellor, as the then head of the judiciary, wielded considerable power behind the scenes with regard to the advancement or otherwise of lawyers and judges.

There was also, either by convention or 'understanding' (but for reasons that might defy any written constitution), a level of permanence about his or her own appointment. A Lord Chancellor was perhaps less likely than a home secretary (or other minister of state) to be 'moved on' in response to some crisis of events; and to an extent, his[1] functions, activities and powers might be obfuscated by processes and procedures that could defy explanation, transparency or any real forms of accountability. This mix of permanence, control of judicial and legal careers[2] together with his central role and influence within Parliament itself (sitting on the Woolsack in the House of Lords) and the fact that, until 2005, he could sit as a judge, simply added to an aura of power. In terms of efficiency, many a decision simply awaited the decision of the Lord Chancellor and going well back in time it was once commented that the law itself might vary with the length of the Lord Chancellor's foot.

A constitutional anomaly

Over and above the way in which the office of Lord Chancellor may have been carried out by individual office holders, in modern times it had become obvious to many commentators that the office had always been a constitutional anomaly. It involved significant elements of all three arms of state, executive, legislative and judicial; although until the Human Rights Act 1998 the murmurings of disapproval may often have been perceived as an attack on the status quo from more radical, rather than more constitutionally aware, quarters. The role was

---

[1] As at 2007, all Lord Chancellors have been men.
[2] Since almost all judges came from the bar and, later, the ranks of solicitors.

reformed in line with constitutional considerations and European obligations. The Constitutional Reform Act 2005 referred to in earlier chapters can be viewed as an acknowledgement by the UK Government that, finally and despite what might be described as idiosyncratic ways of doing things, the tripartite role of the Lord Chancellor was unsound and unsustainable. Hence the new arrangements in relation to the role of Lord Chancellor and new mechanisms in relation to the judiciary such as the Judicial Office, Judicial Appointments Commission, Office of Judicial Complaints and The Concordat between the Lord Chief Justice and Lord Chancellor described in *Chapter 2*. At the same time, the Lord Chancellor was removed from the Woolsack, to be replaced by a Speaker of the House of Lords (similar to that of the House of Commons); and the Lord Chancellor is no longer able to sit as a judge – something that the more 'judicially-inclined' Lord Chancellors did in the past.[3]

The Lord Chancellor is now a minister like any other, with no special attributes or multiple strands of responsibility across government, Parliament and the judiciary. He or she carries what has now become a substantial burden of administrative responsibilities, but seems also to be someone on whom certain duties to safeguard and protect high constitutional principle of the kind described in *Chapter 6* appear to have been cast. As already indicated in *Chapter 1*, the incoming 2007 Lord Chancellor, Jack Straw, immediately – and at a time of significant judicial concern about the arbitrary low key way in which the MOJ had been created – laid great emphasis on his duty to protect the independence of the judiciary, which, so he stated, was his 'first priority'. So too, it seems, the Lord Chancellor must within his or her other scheme of priorities seek to protect the foundations of democracy on which governmental, Parliamentary and judicial institutions all rest.

Ongoing reform

Taken alongside these developments, the creation of the Parliamentary Select Committee on Constitutional Affairs noted in *Chapter 6* has opened up the way to new and higher levels of scrutiny and accountability than formerly existed; and it seems to be relatively clear from *The Governance of Britain*[4] that ongoing reforms, ostensibly encompassing visions, values, transparency, accountability and openness could become the order of the day – integral to the very role of Lord Chancellor, since it is he or she that has been charged with promulgating and presumably upholding them. At the same time, the Lord Chancellor has

---

[3] Lord Hailsham was particularly active in this regard. Any glance through older law reports of cases in the House of Lords reveals that many Lord Chancellors did so and without any apparent sense of concern that they were also part of the Cabinet.

[4] Cm 7170. This Green Paper is mentioned in several earlier chapters and extracts appear in *Appendix IV* to this work.

become an 'ordinary' minister of state; not necessarily, in future, a legally qualified one;[5] and seemingly exposed to the political wind in much the same way all other politicians are. He or she has become a spokesman for the MOJ in a more everyday and maybe less grandiose sense.

THE TITLE OF LORD CHANCELLOR

As noted in *Chapter 1* and to give the head of the MOJ his or her full title, is now styled Secretary of State for Justice and Lord Chancellor, in line with modern developments and the historic origins of former duties and responsibilities. The term 'Justice Minister' or 'Minister for Justice' is also often used, although the latter, especially, would appear also seem to have been reserved for or applied to junior ministers at the MOJ who are charged with the most directly justice-related responsibilities. Whether the somewhat cumbersome new double-barrelled description that appears repeatedly in most of the emerging MOJ pronouncements, on the MOJ web-site and in other official publications, will survive in this form remains to be seen. In this context it is worth noting that an attempt was made by the Government around the time of the Constitutional Reform Act 2005 to simply 'do away' with the ancient office of Lord Chancellor, or at least that title. This was presented as a *fait accompli* by prime minister Tony Blair; a move that was withdrawn when it proved to be unworkable without supporting legislation and administrative arrangements and in the face of an outcry from the judicial and legal community - and also to an extent from politicians who perhaps felt that events were moving too quickly, or that maybe it was unclear where matters were heading. With hindsight it appears that there may already have been an unpublicised MOJ blueprint.

The Lord Chancellor is dead: long live the Lord Chancellor
Given the above events, there is obviously still a sense that holding onto the past by dint of a now long and cumbersome title is worthwhile; and it is doubly understandable that Government would not have wished to be seen to be doing away with the role of Lord Chancellor at the same time that it was busy creating an MOJ. The overtones may have been too sinister. But that which could not be accomplished by what appears to have been a use of the Royal prerogative in 2005, could now occur by a side wind as the description 'Lord Chancellor'

---

5   Jack Straw, the first new-style Lord Chancellor, is, so it happens, a barrister. There is a sense from other MOJ pronouncements that lawyers (or other practitioners) should not think that they own the courts, the law or the justice system; just as politicians do not own democratic institutions. Such nuances appear in *The Governance of Britain* and can perhaps be viewed at one extreme as a response to past situations in which strategies may sometime have been built around what worked best for people within the system.

simply falls away over time in favour of 'Secretary of State for Justice'. The former description would now seem to be titular only.[6] Perhaps it was also the Government's earlier 'bad experience' that underlay the assertion by the MOJ at the time of its creation that 'the role and responsibilities of the Lord Chancellor will not change'. This must be understood in the light of the fact that it has already changed considerably, including quite substantially so under the 2005 Act (above) but also via external symbols, the gradual dispensing with of pomp, ceremony and official costume.

A new kind of political stature

Arguably, the new-style Lord Chancellor will grow in political stature. It can be suggested that the creation of a MOJ not only builds on the 2005 reforms but represents a logical next step towards both transforming and improving the justice system whilst modernising the role of its head as one of the most significant politicians within the Cabinet (and within Cabinet committees of the kind described in *Chapter 1*). Here, it seems, one problem may be that he or she will need to avoid dominating events in a world in which law and order and enforcement have come to the fore, in a way that could alienate people from within the wide range of organizations that now look to the Lord Chancellor as 'their' political reference point, many of which, such as the National Probation Service (NPS) (*Chapter 3*) and Independent Monitoring Boards (IMBs) (*Chapter 4*), have developed from liberal, philanthropic, tolerant and understanding roots (*Chapter 3*). Whatever may be the merits of progress, it will be important to retain something of the inherent identity of these and other agencies in terms of both that background and the sometimes considerable ways in which they have 'reinvented' themselves in modern times in order to recognise the need for new priorities, standards, performance and delivery. This may involve a quite different kind of balancing exercise within the mind of the Lord Chancellor from that which will be needed in relation to the judiciary.

Dispensing with the past

Dispensing with the past is very much part of the modern way of government. History has sometimes been given a bad name or even blackened, where it was thought to stand in the way of progress. There is, seemingly, a strange irony in

---

[6] It is not wholly clear whether the title has been retained due to a mix of deference to sensitive feelings and sentimentality or whether some (possibly obscure) legal nicety means that the description would need to continue pending statutory or other Parliamentary attention and provisions. The events of 2005 suggest that the latter is not the position. What is clear is that the Lord Chancellor need no longer be a member of the House of Lords so that there is no pressing reason to retain the pre-fix 'lord'.

the retention of 'Lord Chancellor' as part of the title of the MOJ's new-style head by a Government that has sometimes been dismissive of what history or experience has to offer. This has also gone hand-in-hand with legislative reforms that have done away with or adapted what until recent years many judges, lawyers and commentators saw as fundamental principle, or even sacrosanct. Much of this has occurred in statutes whose contents have been too numerous and complex to comprehend.[7] What seems to matter most, is that significant aspects of professional cultures and the values of practitioners, often built up over many years, should not evaporate as part of any such debunking process.

Much, it might be suggested, will in future depend on the strength and to some extent the ingenuity of whoever is in charge of the MOJ and upon his or her understanding of the need to preserve that which has stood the test of time; as well as protecting checks and balances, whether in relation to the citizen and the state, in order to underpin judicial independence, or to properly facilitate interdependent decision-making across the justice process.

PRESSURE POINTS FOR ANY LORD CHANCELLOR

In sustaining constitutional reforms whilst also managing the wide agenda of justice-related responsibilities, there are bound to be points of pressure and tension of which the following scenarios may be indicative. In playing a key role in the Cabinet and its various (and seemingly developing) committees and dealing with the various services and organizations that are linked to the MOJ, the Lord Chancellor:

- will need to consider how far his or her proximity to justice-related functions may conflict with other Government priorities and the extent that resistance will be possible when dealing closely and ostensibly alongside and in tandem with other ministers such as the home secretary and prime minister in particular;
- may need to consider how far the MOJ's key aim of preventing and reducing crime may sometimes be in conflict with its role in relation to the delivery of criminal justice and human rights, which overall would seem to place him or her at the self-same time in the position of pursuing offenders and people involved in crime and anti-social behaviour whilst also making sure, via the judiciary, that they receive a fair trial and, if they are convicted, that they receive a proportionate and consistent sentence;

---

[7] For some comments in relation to criminal justice, see *Chapter 10* of the companion to this work, *The New Home Office*. But it is not just criminal justice: wide scale and complex reforms have been occurring virtually across-the-board.

- could find himself or herself needing to make difficult resource decisions which would have the effect of impacting on the work of the courts or other services, a prime example of which is provided by the need to accommodate people in prisons without unduly influencing – or in roundabout ways constraining – the nature and quality of judicial decision-making;

- may find himself or herself too close to events where the MOJ or one of its many linked services, agencies or sponsored organizations is involved in court-related or tribunal-related proceedings, so that conflict begins to seep into the MOJ itself; and

- may need to create mechanisms to prevent, e.g. his or her shared aims with other government departments beginning to play too forceful a role in relation to the research, statistics, data, information and proposals that he or she may bring to the Sentencing Guidelines Council (SGC) (*Chapter 3*) or in relation to The Concordat with the Lord Chief Justice (also *Chapter 3*).

It has already become clear that the MOJ is a new department of state, not simply the old LCD or DCA with new functions added. It will need to establish its own identity and professional culture, its own relationships, and what will in due course become its own traditions. It has been established at a time when the reforms of government and of public service which had been accumulating over the past 25 years were beginning to move from a series of rapid changes in legislation and organization; some of which did little more than re-arrange the furniture, to a transformation of the character of British government and governance, in its relationships with public services and public servants, and in the relationships of both with UK citizens. Social and economic changes were at the same time affecting the character of British society. The transformation was by no means complete, and continuing change and adjustment seems more likely, and more to be hoped for, than a static, settled state.

The epicentre of change
The Lord Chancellor will be at the centre of the processes of change that are now taking place. He or she will be involved at a political, professional and practical level in carrying through and sometimes correcting the continuing reforms of criminal and civil justice and of the country's constitutional arrangements – and along with the MOJ and its senior officials will be involved at a strategic level in resolving the inevitable tensions between human rights and public protection and in providing reassurance for people who feel angry, fearful or frustrated by what they may see going on around them.

For all the dignity and splendour of their office, few Lord Chancellors (apart perhaps from Thomas Wolsey) have left a lasting imprint on British or

English history. New-style Lord Chancellors, ministers of justice and their officials are likely to be much more involved in the life of the nation than most old-style Lord Chancellors ever were, with more opportunities for influencing events and greater responsibilities to carry out that will touch upon ordinary lives than they might ever have expected or previously experienced. Those opportunities and responsibilities will make special demands upon political and professional skills, judgement, personal resolve and strength of character. Given the move towards joined-up Cabinet committee-style government, Lord Chancellors may frequently need to stand up to the prime minister and home secretary, as when, e.g. the debate turns to finding ever increasing ways of fast-tracking aspects of the justice system. Historically, the Lord Chancellor was also the Keeper of the Great Seal, the main symbol of the authority of the sovereign. The new-style Lord Chancellor may well find that he or she will need to be the Keeper of the Nation's Conscience.

CHAPTER 10

Into a Fresh Era

CHAPTER 10

Into a New Era

This book began with a brief reference to the speed of events whereby the Ministry of Justice (MOJ) came into being on 9 May 2007, virtually as a *fait accompli*, following an earlier revelation by the then Home Secretary, Dr John Reid, that the then Department of Constitutional Affair's (DCA's) longstanding partner in government, the Home Office, was 'not fit for purpose'.

THE SPEED AND NATURE OF EVENTS

Ahead of the events of May 2007, there was little or no public debate, discussion, scrutiny, consultation or ceremony concerning the MOJ. This contrasts with certain developments described in parts of this book where, in relation to certain new measures (such as forthcoming Criminal Justice Bills) there was extensive prior consultation and debate. Historically, measures of far less import had been scrutinised much more closely. Even the vast majority of judges and magistrates were taken by surprise. With hindsight, Dr Reid's revelatory 'not fit for purpose' moment can perhaps be seen as indicative of the fact that moves to split up the Home Office and transfer out certain of its functions were already well afoot.[1] The judiciary in particular were taken aback – to the extent that temporary working arrangements needed to be agreed between the Lord Chief Justice and Lord Chancellor to pre-empt what according to the media might have become the UK's first mass 'walk out' by judges.[2] The idea of an MOJ had been mentioned several times in Cabinet committees, but not with the kind of emphasis that would ordinarily have led people, even those close to events, to think that such a major reshaping of Government was imminent. Yet the MOJ appeared on its first day complete with a new livery, a well-appointed headquarters, instant publications in support and a well-constructed and informative web-site.[3] None of this could possibly have occurred overnight.

A logical progression
It was sometimes a shallow boast of some UK-based commentators that, in contrast to the situation in many foreign jurisdictions, the UK had neither an

---

[1] For the longer background to functions being 'transferred out' of the burgeoning Home Office, see the companion to this work, *The New Home Office*.

[2] See, also, in this regard comments already made in *Chapter 3*.

[3] www.justice.gov.uk

MOJ nor a (more ominous sounding) Ministry of the Interior. It has now – the former in fact (and the subject of this book) and the latter by way of a descriptive tag regularly applied to the new-style, sleeker, public safety and law and order-oriented Home Office. That the UK was about to enter a new era became clearer on a change of premiership and rapidly afterwards when the Green Paper, *The Governance of Britain*[4] – which again could not have been thought out and written in a short time frame – was issued, inviting views on a wide range of constitutional, democratic, judicial and associated issues (see, especially, *Chapter 6*).

What emerges from this is the MOJ as an integral part, indeed the central component in, enhanced arrangements for constitutional and justice-related arrangements in the UK, possibly extending to a new constitution (and even a written constitution). Seen via a lens trained on the Constitutional Reform Act 2005 and other developments of a kind mentioned in earlier chapters of this book, the 2007 reforms are thrown into relief and can be viewed as a logical progression. But it would be remiss to end this book, however basic its aims, without some further comment, if for no other reason than that the new MOJ prides itself on transparency and openness.

A lack of ceremony and engagement

Over and above a lack of ceremony, there was a lack of visibility and public (as well as judicial) engagement. In this, the birth of the MOJ represents an inauspicious start for a department that prides itself on openness and accountability, even if some commentators since appear to have warmed to many of the more democratic sentiments within *The Governance of Britain*, its flagship document. The events barely made the main news on most TV channels and radio stations; often by way of an afterthought in a report about forthcoming sentencing changes. On the morning after the development was announced there were small items in *The Times* (on page 21) and *Guardian* (page 14).[5] At the time most media attention was heavily distracted by the fact that the then prime minister, Tony Blair, was expected to declare when he would leave office

---

[4] Cm 7170. Also, it would seem, longer in the making than might at first appear from the instant creation of the MOJ, such is that document's depth, erudition and reach. The Foreword, Executive summary and Introduction appear in *Appendix VI* to this work. The sophistication of *Justice: A New Approach* (2007) (MOJ 1/07) and *Penal Policy: A Background Paper* (2007) (MOJ 1/0) (with NOMS) two 'first-day' publications of the MOJ, also suggest that the MOJ was in embryo at the time of Dr Reid's revelatory 'not fit for purpose' moment. Rather, it looks as though, politically speaking, May 2007 was an opportunity not to be missed and Dr Reid's comments a device to accelerate matters.

[5] In an edition that devoted more space to a piece about the former East German Stasi and modern deployment of an invention for piecing together shredded documents.

(though to be fair both *The Times* and *Guardian* had earlier trailed the prospect of an MOJ without knowing exactly what it might entail and the latter did make an editorial comment). The events made it into the *Sun* newspaper at the top of page 2, but only as part of a scathing piece about 'bumbling Lord Falconer' who was accused of being 'soft on crime'. This on his first day in office at the MOJ, having just inherited the National Offender Management Service (NOMS) and having hardly had time to read his brief and get to grips with the impact of prison recall on prison overcrowding – a problem bequeathed to him by Dr Reid.[6]

The BBC2 TV *Newsnight* programme seems to have been one of the few media outlets to have given the new arrangements the attention they deserved, or to recognise their constitutional significance and potential for dysfunction. Film footage was shown of the assembled judiciary, row upon row, po-faced, described as being 'angry' that mechanisms to protect judicial independence had not been adequately considered beforehand. Within days, any chance of sustained news value that might have attached to the Home Office split/MOJ had been swept away in the tsunami of coverage of the then Blair/Brown handover-cum-Labour leadership election campaign.

Some immediate reactions

But there was time for some responses. On the day that the MOJ was announced, David Cameron MP, leader of the Tory Opposition, speaking in the House of Commons, described the final days of Tony Blair's administration as 'a Government of the living dead', but one yet determined to push through a plethora of reforms to underwrite the 'Blair legacy', of which the MOJ was an example. David Davis, shadow spokesman on Home Affairs went further in describing the new arrangements as 'a dog's breakfast'.

There were more considered criticisms concerning the scope for conflict, e.g. if the courts and judiciary had to compete with other justice agencies, especially with prisons, for their funding. At that moment, few outsiders could have known much about the well-worked arrangements that had obviously been put together

---

[6] Lord Falconer had announced a proposal to limit run-of-the-mill recall of released prisoners to 28 days at a time, which seems to have been wilfully misinterpreted, in some reports, so as to suggest that he was seeking to alter a wide range of sentences. The *Sun* noted that Lord Falconer would now 'almost certainly be sacked' by Gordon Brown if he became prime minister; though, possibly, like Dr Reid, Lord Falconer had already indicated that he would leave office if and when Tony Blair gave up being prime minister. Other accounts claimed that he was 'fighting to keep his job' and still others that he was working hard to see in the new-MOJ. Somewhat questionably, the *Sun* also ran an editorial headed 'Sack Charlie [Falconer]' which it described as an 'urgent priority' and whom it described as a 'warbling clot'. This from what BBC2 TV *Newsnight* maintains is 'the most influential newspaper in Britain'.

behind the scenes, courtesy of a corps of civil servants it has to be assumed. In the preceding days, Lord Phillips of Worth Matravers, Lord Chief Justice, had referred to various 'matters of principle' that stood to be resolved and this was reflected by the *Guardian* in its editorial comment (May 10):

> The unresolved 'issues of principle' that the Lord Chief Justice alluded to, boil down to three concerns. First, money: the judges are worried that the courts will now have to compete for funding directly with the political priority of prisons. Second, judges fear the loss of the direct link to the cabinet which the Lord Chancellor traditionally provided, especially if future justice secretaries are elected politicians with no legal training. Finally that the desire to curry favour could contaminate judgements, when, as in prison law, the justice secretary might be the respondent.

Hopefully, the foregoing chapters of this book, admittedly written at a greater distance in time and on the basis of information that has come to the fore subsequently, indicate the far wider implications of and background to such changes. Nonetheless, it is interesting to note that the overall tone was constructive, supportive and conciliatory, again, typified by the *Guardian's* editorial which noted that such:

> ... objections are not insurmountable, for combined justice ministries work well overseas. And [the judges'] caution may be excessive – as it was when the lord chancellor's role was reformed, in a move that has turned out to strengthen rather than weaken judicial independence. As long as court funds are ring-fenced and there are rules of law, bringing elected ministers into the administration of justice will be a welcome and democratic step.

It is also interesting to note, in contrast to the coverage of many political events of modern times, that support has tended to be maintained – at least from the broadsheets. Anecdotally, it was as if the general public was looking to more settled or less overtly troublesome political times.

But the media was also quick to note that both John Reid and Lord Falconer were set to depart and the phenomenon whereby key political changes are set in train by someone who then leaves matters to his or her successor was described by one commentator as 'breaking eggs but without making the omelette', something that makes ongoing public scrutiny more difficult.

Earlier events

A Government backlash against difficulties experienced from the 1980s onwards in seeking to achieve relatively modest aspects of constitutional change, led to the creation of the then Department of Constitution Affairs (DCA) and other new arrangements that followed, as described in *Chapter 6*. But in thinking of an MOJ, most commentators probably felt that the word 'justice' signified courts, judges, magistrates, and maybe tribunals along with other directly and identifiably justice-related matters and issues of the kind noted in *Chapter 2*. They may have also have preferred a more dignified and inclusive approach when a different kind of animal began to appear. Few judges might have expected, e.g. that they would, in effect, become part of an MOJ that is in the nature of a criminal justice multi-agency partnership;[7] and at a time when (so it seems) the standing of and trust in politicians must have been close to an all time low.

IMPROVING THE JUSTICE SYSTEM

Yet it would be unfair, at least for the time being, not to be constructive and to give the new arrangements the benefit of any doubts or concerns. Thus, e.g. it can be noted that, before leaving office, Lord Falconer intimated that the MOJ exists for 'one purpose and one purpose only' - that is 'to improve the justice system':

> The MOJ provides the opportunity for the whole justice system to work together better than ever before. The justice system is here to serve the public and we must give the public the system it deserves. Justice needs a Ministry of Justice.

Rhetoric and circularity worthy perhaps of a latter-day George Orwell – but the modern way of Government and in line with the elusive and insubstantial nature of many assertions to emanate from across government departments of late. Hence, also, the deceptive simplicity of the MOJ's stated aims noted in *Chapter 1*, that, in reality, do not explain a great deal about what the MOJ will actually do. Hopefully, e.g. 'sense in sentencing' is coded language for better use of the Sentencing Guidelines Council (SGC) and the Sentencing Advisory Panel (SAP) (which will now hear from a minister for justice rather than a home secretary *Chapter 7*). Similarly, 'serving the public', a central tenet of the MOJ's general aims, sits alongside other imprecise objectives such as 'less re-offending', 'public confidence that the punishment fits the crime', 'connection to communities' and 'victims feeling [that] the system looks after them'. One early assurance was that the UK would have 'a system of justice of which we can be rightly proud . . . admired around the world'. Impressive language which many citizens may agree with. But on closer examination, with what exactly?

---

[7] There is no guarantee that the MOJ will survive long term or in its present form. The Opposition has already indicated that it would abolish the MOJ if it came to power before the MOJ becomes too entrenched.

A clean sheet

The great benefit of any new organization whether in the public sector, private sector or voluntary sector is that it begins with a clean sheet and an absence of what is usually called 'baggage' (or baggage that can be discarded as being that of a predecessor). In *Justice: A New Approach*, the MOJ sets out the ways that it will actively 'promote justice', i.e. 'by:

- ensuring that our justice system is accessible and effective, respected and understood;
- continuing to modernise the institutions and systems that serve the justice system;
- putting into practice principles of justice and respect for the rule of law throughout all public services and institutions;
- setting standards for equality and fairness, and ensuring that the justice system is reflective of the communities it serves;
- ensuring that offenders are managed effectively and that the sentence of the court is delivered;
- ensuring that better outcomes for children remains the essential role of the Family Justice System and that parties in civil disputes are given proportionate ways to resolve their disagreements.'

What seems to be important here is that the flexibility and occasional vagueness that are in inherent in such broad brush assertions are not allowed to impact on those fundamental values that are intrinsic to constitutional affairs or justice. At one time, Lord Falconer used the phrase 'doing justice differently'. For people who regard justice as a static or inherently unchanging concept, encompassing matters such as fairness, consistency and proportionality, this might be viewed as a hazardous use of language. Better, perhaps, not to talk about different ways of doing justice (which could of course also be better or worse ways); as opposed to new and improved mechanisms for – or a new approach to – that which is to be delivered. Within the judiciary, in particular, there is likely to be continuing debate and watchfulness concerning the idea that justice can be altered and whether the MOJ does represent 'a better way'.

Similarly, such notions as community involvement in justice also require scrutiny. Taken alongside suggestions that have been to the fore in recent years, there is always the prospect that the MOJ could become the vehicle for competing forms of justice: less expensive, slicker and not so legalistic or complicated as that which requires judges, juries and magistrates.[8] That could be

---

[8] From a different perspective, some commentators have argued that such developments are a way of putting judges and other criminal justice practitioners under pressure to be

an illusory 'bargain'; and, as, e.g. outwardly simple things like the rise of the anti-social behaviour order (or ASBO) demonstrate, from small acorns large oak trees can quickly grow; the same way that police community support officers (PCSOs) have come to replace police officers proper on the streets in many places, and with expanded powers.[9] Justice is now fast-tracked in all kinds of directions; the powers of the police, courts and tribunals have grown enormously. Examples of the way in which public institutions have (sometimes almost imperceptibly) changed and often increased in power right across government in the past ten years are legion. There is perhaps no better time for a review of fundamentals.

ISSUES AND CHALLENGES FOR THE MOJ

The Green Paper *The Governance of Britain* announced in July 2007 represents just such a review as intimated already at various points in this book. Its broad content can be seen from *Appendix IV* to this work. What seems to be important in such exercises is that consultation (see, generally, *Chapter 8*) should be a matter of listening and learning, not of telling and selling, and still less of facing-down criticism. Citizens, including MOJ and other government staff, should feel that their opinions and experience are understood and valued. If not, they will detach themselves from the process.[10] The purpose of consultation has too often been, or has been perceived as being, to explain and gain support for what the Government has already decided rather than to hear and take account of alternative proposals or different points of view.

Where criticism *has* been expressed, it has often been treated as evidence of unreliability or disloyalty (as with developments in relation to NOMS perhaps), or the person has been portrayed as being 'on the wrong side' – in favour, e.g. of criminals or against victims or hardworking people in general. The limits of the debate should not be so narrowly defined that discussion is restricted to technicalities rather than to real principle.[11] It may not be possible to obtain total agreement or support, but those who have worked hard or whose lives may be affected should feel that they have been listened to, that what they said has been taken seriously, and that they have been treated with respect. Whether or not *The*

---

more repressive, because that is what communities will want. There are elements of the hue and cry of former times.

[9] See the companion volume to this work, *The New Home Office,* Chapter 3.

[10] See, e.g. 'Experiencing Modernisation: Frontline Probation Perspectives on the Transition to a National Offender Management Service' (2007), Robinson, G and Burnett, R, *Probation Journal,* forthcoming,

[11] As it was, e.g. in consultations on a proposal, later abandoned, for a combined inspectorate for the Criminal Justice System in (2005) or a prisoner's right to vote (2007).

Governance of Britain represents the gateway to a new and refreshing era of consultation and democratic accountability, various points can be suggested that the Lord Chancellor and MOJ might do well to ponder as part of any rethinking that is about to occur:

- the role and scope of the criminal law, as well as the potential for looking towards non-criminal ways of resolving situations;
- the structure of sentencing, the role of the Sentencing Guidelines Council, (SGC), and the relationship between NOMS and the courts, and the courts' real responsibilities in relation to sentencing;
- the commissioning process for services, facilities and resources and their overall dynamics;
- the structures, relationships, contracts and responsibilities with regard to offender management;
- relationships and human values: how relationships and experiences can change behaviour, issues of motivation, responsibility, opportunity, restoration and reconciliation;
- accountability in terms of central and local ownership;
- measuring, or judging , success in terms of the delivery of policies;
- staff leadership, management, professional standards and values;
- the science and legitimacy of risk assessment and 'what works' in terms of crime prevention and crime reduction;
- science and technology and its uses and limitations (practical and ethical) in improving democracy and all its institutions;
- research: how it is commissioned and applied; and
- various cross-cutting themes that affect a range of matters or issues – such as restorative justice, community justice, race, religion and those affecting to victims and witnesses.

All this will occur within the broader framework and ethos of the MOJ and Government generally. And so it is perhaps worth recording one key passage from *The Governance of Britain*, which sets the context within which the Lord Chancellor and MOJ will need to operate:

> The Government wants to ensure that the powers that it holds are legitimately owned and fairly used … [It] will be consulting on how best to ensure that it has appropriate authority and no more than is required. In the UK's system, the separation of powers ensures that no one institution can wield too much influence over the others: Parliament, the executive and the judiciary balance each other. It is an organic relationship which evolves and requires continual review.[12]

---

[12] Cm 7170; paragraph 86.

Appendix I *The United Kingdom Constitution*[1]

Although the bedrock of personal liberties in Britain is traditionally held to be Magna Carta, the birth of the modern British constitution is often considered to be the Glorious Revolution of 1688. The deposition of James II of England and James VII of Scotland led to the beginnings of a parliamentary democracy in which no Monarch could wield absolute power. The Parliaments of England and Scotland enacted in quick succession the legislation that still forms the basis of the relationship between Monarchy and Parliament and between Parliament and people. The English Declaration of Rights 1689 and the Scottish Claim of Right Act 1689 set out the roles of Parliament and of the Crown, and also the fundamental rights of the people – for example, to be subject to proper justice, and free from military rule or excessive fines. The intervention of Parliament in 1688 and then in 1700 to determine the succession to the Crown was an indication of how far, by that time, power had shifted from the Monarch to Parliament. The Treaty of Union 1706, enacted by the Parliaments of England and Scotland in 1707, created Britain as a nation. The settlement put into place at the beginning of the 18th century was sufficiently flexible and adaptable to accommodate significant further shifts in power and responsibility within the Government. The 18th century was therefore a period of constitutional consolidation and evolutionary development. Although it saw dramatic developments elsewhere, such as the loss of the American colonies, and the wars against revolutionary France, in Britain there was no further dramatic change. The Union with Ireland Act in 1800 was the only decisive constitutional statute.

It was not until the 1830s that the system came under such strain that formal legislative intervention was needed. As a result of the industrial revolution, the pattern of the electoral franchise – the law governing who can vote – had become untenable. Large centres of population had no MPs, while some deserted villages returned two. The franchise was extended by the Great Reform Act 1832, but the type of elector and the type of person who was elected changed little. This was, therefore, only the first step on a road of electoral reform which culminated in the introduction of universal adult franchise nearly a century later, in 1928. Just as power had passed from the Crown to Parliament, and from Ministers selected by the King to Ministers endorsed by Parliament, so power also gradually passed from the House of Lords to the House of Commons. The extension of the franchise, the increasing scope of government and the consequent need for public funding, gradually consolidated the Commons' position. When the House of Lords rejected Lloyd George's budget in 1909, they were already breaching a convention of some years' standing. The result of their action was the Parliament

---

[1] Source: *The Governance of Britain*

Act 1911, which finally confirmed the superiority of the Commons. The Act, as amended in 1949, still governs the relationship between the two Houses.

The first half of the 20th century also saw the partition of Ireland (in 1921) and the transition from Empire to Commonwealth. The second half of the 20th century saw constitutional reform across Europe which recast the relationship between the citizen and the state and the relationship between nation states and the broader international community. In Britain, the 1945 Labour Government established the welfare state, building on the reforms of the 1906 Liberal Government. British citizens gained a range of economic and social rights, like universal access to healthcare. The decision to give home rule to India in 1947 was only part of a process in which Britain changes its relationship with peoples and territories across the globe, as new nation states emerged, often in bloody struggle, from former European colonial empires. The post-war settlement also saw the growth in international organisations and international conceptions of rights. The establishment of the United Nations in 1945 led to the Universal Declaration of Human Rights (1948), which in turn inspired two major UN human rights treaties, the International Covenant on Civil and Political Rights and the International Covenant on Economic, Social and Cultural Rights (both 1966); the UK is party to each. The Treaty of London (1949) created the Council of Europe, which now has 47 member states and works to promote democracy, human rights and the rule of law. Under its auspices, the European Convention on Human Rights (1950) was drafted principally by British lawyers and in 1973 the UK joined the European Economic Community (now the European Union) and became a part of a multinational political structure. Post-war electoral reforms continued the process of promoting fairness. These reforms included the abolition of plural voting in 1948, which meant that electors could vote only in their constituency, and the reduction of the voting age to 18 in 1969. The Life Peerages Act 1958 allowed the creation of many non-hereditary members of the House of Lords, and also permitted women to sit in the House of Lords for the first time. The Peerage Act 1963 allowed hereditary peers to renounce their titles to remain in the House of Commons. Local government saw a number of reforms designed to marry democratic accountability with the most efficient delivery of public services. The Local Government Act 1972 introduced the two-tier pattern of county and district councils still used in many parts of England today; however, the metropolitan county councils that it created, along with the Greater London Council (1965), were abolished in 1986. The Local Government Act 1992 allowed the creation of single-tier unitary authorities. Following successive reforms, local government in Wales, Scotland and Northern Ireland now also follows a single-tier model, based on counties and country boroughs (Wales), council areas (Scotland) and districts (Northern Ireland). Through the 1980s and 1990s, government power was devolved to a wide range of bodies, including executive agencies and quangos (today called non-departmental public bodies). Public services that had previously been provided only by national or local government increasingly came to be provided under contract by the private sector. Many major nationalised utilities, including electricity, water and gas, were also privatised, as was British Rail in 1995-7. Also in 1997, the Labour Party returned to power with an agenda for wide-ranging constitutional reform, outlined earlier in this document.

Appendix II *Bodies sponsored by the Ministry of Justice*

Advisory Committees on General Commissioners of Income Tax
Advisory non departmental public body (NDPB)
Role contained in Judicial Appointments annual report 2002

Advisory Committees on General Commissioners of Income Tax (Northern Ireland)
Advisory non departmental public body (NDPB) to Northern Ireland Court Service
Role set out in Judicial Appointments annual report 2002

Advisory Committees on Justices of the Peace in England and Wales
Advisory non departmental public body (NDPB)
Role set out in the 'Becoming a Magistrate'

Advisory Committees on Justices of the Peace in Lancashire, Greater Manchester and Merseyside
Advisory non departmental public body (NDPB)
Role set out in the 'Becoming a Magistrate'

Advisory Council on Historical Manuscripts
Advisory non departmental public body (NDPB) to The National Archives
Role set out in its own terms of reference

Advisory Council on National Records and Archives
Advisory non departmental public body (NDPB) to The National Archives
Role set out in its own terms of reference

Advisory Council on Public Records
Advisory non departmental public body (NDPB) to The National Archives
Role set out in its own terms of reference

Advisory Panel on Public Sector Information
Advisory non departmental public body (NDPB) to The National Archives

Assessor for Compensation for Miscarriages of Justice
Independent Body
Role set out in its own statement

The Boundary Commission, England
Advisory non departmental public body (NDPB)
Role set out in 'Our Role and Responsibilities'

The Boundary Commission, Scotland
Advisory non departmental public body (NDPB) to Scotland Office
Role set out in Fifth Periodical Review
The Boundary Commission, Wales

Advisory non departmental public body (NDPB)
Role set out in annual report 2005/06

Civil Justice Council
Advisory non departmental public body (NDPB)
Role set out in code of practice

Civil Procedure Rule Committee
Advisory non departmental public body (NDPB)

Correctional Services Accreditation Panel
Advisory non departmental public body (NDPB)
Role set out in annual report 2005/06

Council on Tribunals
Advisory non departmental public body (NDPB)
Role set out in functions and constitution

Courts Boards
Advisory non departmental public body (NDPB)
Role set out in Courts Boards guidance

Criminal Cases Review Commission
Executive non departmental public body (NDPB)

Criminal Injuries Compensation Authority
Executive non departmental public body (NDPB)
Role set out in mission statement

Criminal Procedure Rule Committee
Advisory non departmental public body (NDPB)

Crown Court Rule Committee
Advisory non departmental public body (NDPB)
Role set out in terms of reference

The Directorate of Judicial Offices for England and Wales
Independent directorate comprising: the Judicial Office; Judicial Studies Board; and
Judicial Communications Office

Family Justice Council
Advisory non departmental public body (NDPB)
Role set out in terms of reference

Family Procedure Rule Committee
Advisory non departmental public body (NDPB)
Role set out in terms of reference in 2006 annual report.

HM Courts Service (HMCS)
Executive agency
Role set out in framework document

HM Inspectorate of Court Administration
Independent statutory office
Role set out in remit and guiding principles

HM Inspectorate of Prisons
Independent Inspectorate
Role set out in statement of purpose

HM Inspectorate of Probation
Independent Inspectorate
Role set out in statement of purpose

HM Land Registry
Non Ministerial Dept and Trading Fund Executive Agency
Role set out in framework document

HM Prison Service
Executive Agency
Role set out in statement of purpose

Independent Monitoring Boards
Advisory non departmental public body (NDPB)

Insolvency Rules Committee
Advisory non departmental public body (NDPB)
Role set out in its own terms of reference

Judicial Appointments Commission (JAC)
Executive non departmental public body (NDPB)
Role set out in framework document

Judicial Appointments and Conduct Ombudsman
Independent statutory office
Role set out in memorandum of understanding

Land Registration Rule Committee
Advisory non departmental public body (NDPB)
Role set out in freedom of information publication scheme

Law Commission
   Advisory non departmental public body (NDPB)
   Role set out in working practices

Legal Services Commission (LSC)
   Executive non departmental public body (NDPB)
   Role set out in framework document

Legal Services Consultative Panel
   Advisory non departmental public body (NDPB)
   Role set out in work programme 2004/05

The National Archives (TNA)
   Non ministerial department and executive agency
   Role set out in plans and strategy and a framework document (under revision)

National Offender Management Service (NOMS)
   Part of Ministry of Justice corporate centre
   Role set out in 'About NOMS'

National Probation Service
   Independent non departmental public body (NDPB)
   Role set out in its aims and objectives

Northern Ireland Court Service (NiCtS)
   Separate Civil Service
   Role set out in statement of purpose and strategic objectives

Northern Ireland Judicial Appointments Commission
   Executive non departmental public body (NDPB) to Northern Ireland Court Service

Northern Ireland Legal Services Commission
   Executive non departmental public body (NDPB) to Northern Ireland Court Service
   Role set out in mission and aims

Office for Criminal Justice Reform (OCJR)
   Tri-lateral body
   Role set out objectives and responsibilities

Office of the Information Commissioner
   Executive non departmental public body (NDPB)
   Role set out in framework document

Office of the Judge Advocate General
   Independent body

Office of the Judicial Committee
Part of Ministry of Justice, reporting ministerially to the Lord President of the Council
Role set out in objectives and structure

Office for Judicial Complaints
Other independent offices
Role set out in memorandum of understanding

Office of the Legal Services Complaints Commissioner
Independent statutory office
Role set out in role and statutory powers

Office of the Legal Services Ombudsman
Independent statutory office
Role set out in annual report 2005/06

Office of Courts Funds, the Official Solicitor and Public Trustee
Independent statutory office
Role set out in function of the offices

Parliamentary Boundary Commission for England
Advisory non departmental public body (NDPB)
Role set out in code of practice

Parole Board
Executive non departmental public body (NDPB)
Role set out in role of the board

Prisons and Probation Ombudsman
Ombudsman
Role set out in annual report 2005/06

Privy Council Secretariat
Part of Ministry of Justice, reporting ministerially to the Lord President of the Council
Role set out in objectives and structure

Public Guardianship Office (PGO)
Executive agency
Role set out in framework document

Scotland Office
Office relating to devolved administrations
Role set out in memorandum of understanding

Sentencing Advisory Panel
Advisory non departmental public body (NDPB)

Sentencing Guidelines Council
Advisory non departmental public body (NDPB)
Role set out in statement of purpose

Strategic Investment Board
Advisory non departmental public body (NDPB)
Role set out in terms of reference

Tribunals Service
Executive agency
Role set out in framework document

Victims Advisory Panel
Advisory non departmental public body (NDPB)

Wales Office
Office relating to devolved administrations
Role set out in memorandum of understanding

Youth Justice Board for England and Wales
Executive non departmental public body (NDPB)
Role set out in 'Our mission'.

Appendix III *The Courts of Law*

The following is a basic outline of some of the main courts of law in England and Wales, together with a description of their judges, and can usefully be read in conjunction with *Chapter 2*, in particular.

Magistrates' courts
Magistrates' courts deal with over with 2.3 million defendants in criminal cases a year and 1.2 million civil applications.[2] All criminal cases start out (are 'commenced') in the magistrates' court, except in certain rare situations whereby a case can start in the Crown Court by way of what is known as a voluntary bill of indictment, or where some extra item is attached to existing proceedings that have already reached the Crown Court.

However, in modern times and in the most serious cases the role of the magistrates' court is confined to dealing with the initial remand proceedings and associated matters such as legal aid before the case is committed or transferred straightaway to the Crown Court. That court then takes responsibility for the future conduct of the case, including decisions from then onwards about whether the accused person will be held in custody (usually meaning on remand in prison in the case of an adult)[3] pending his or her trial. The magistrates' courts are served by volunteer justices of the peace (unpaid but trained) or by a professional 'district judge (magistrates' courts)'.

Youth courts
The MOJ retains responsibility for the Youth Justice Board (YJB), created by the Crime and Disorder Act 1998, and the Ministry of Justice (MOJ) now shares oversight of youth justice with the new Department for Children, Schools and Families as described in the main text.

The MOJ has commented on the 'radical overhaul' that has already taken place concerning the way that children and young people who offend are managed. It noted that over the last ten years this had been characterised 'by the success of Youth Offending Teams (YOTs): multi-agency bodies of local authorities that have been established in every area, 'leading to young offenders being dealt with more quickly and being more likely to make amends for their wrongdoing':

> The cornerstone of our approach will remain investment in early intervention and prevention. We aim to reduce the number of first-time entrants into the Criminal Justice System. This will require a multi-agency approach with schools, police, health

---

[2] 2006.

[3] Or even a 17-year-old who is subject to adult procedures for this purpose.

services, etc., working together to early identify children at risk of offending and to intervene effectively ...

We will continue to focus our efforts on increasing the number of pre-court diversions designed to keep children out of the Criminal Justice System. Getting a young person to acknowledge the harm they have caused face to face and make amends is an important part of their learning and critical to improving victim confidence in the system.

As the MOJ notes, there will always be a number of children whose offending behaviour means that they must go to court. Youth courts have seen a 26 per cent increase in business since 2002, which is making it more difficult for sentencers to keep a grip on individuals. 'Our aim is to build on the lessons learned from the CJS Simple Speedy Summary justice programme in the adult court and look at how we can speed up and improve processes in the youth court – case handling needs to be efficient, fast and fair. Communities should be involved wherever possible, building on community panel arrangements for referral orders[4] as well as ensuring victims have a say. Of the children who reach court, a very small number will end up in custody because of the need to protect the public, which remains paramount. However, the MOJ asserts that custody must remain the last resort for children'. Youth courts are served by youth court magistrates (a panel of the magistrates' court, above), or in some instances by district judges.

The Crown Court
The Crown Court replaced the former and historic courts of Assize and Quarter Sessions in 1972 under the Courts Act 1971. Principally the role of the Crown Court is to deal with trials before a judge and jury with regard to what are known as indictable cases, i.e. those which can or must be tried in this way because they are either 'indictable only' (the most serious, such as murder, rape, terrorism, serious sexual offences) or 'triable either way' (meaning either in the magistrates court or the Crown Court depending on the outcome of a procedure known as 'mode of trial' as part of which the accused person can elect to be tried by a jury).[5] In 2006/07 the Crown Courts disposed of 127,751 hearings or trials. They are served mainly by circuit judges or part-time circuit judges, often

---

[4] Under which those appearing in the youth court for the first time are normally referred to a community panel to devise a plan for the juvenile in conjunction with the YOT to avoid a sentence proper, wherever possible.

[5] There are variations and nuances. In its simplest form, mode of trial involves the court in deciding whether or not the case is suitable for summary trial, i.e. trial in the magistrates' court depending, e.g. on its seriousness and complexity; but the accused person still has an unfettered right to jury trial. Complications exist re a procedure known as 'plea before venue' as to which, other works should be consulted.

described as 'recorders'. Members of the higher judiciary usually sit to deal with the most serious cases, again with a jury.[6] The presiding judge of a Crown Court or its circuit is generally a High Court judge.

The High Court
The High Court is based in The Strand in London but may also sit at other venues in the UK. It consists of the Queen's Bench Division, Civil Division, Chancery Division and Family Division each of which has its own jurisdiction. It also deals with judicial review of administrative action or of a decision of a lower court where that route of 'appeal' is chosen by the applicant and is legally appropriate. The High Court is served by High Court judges. A Divisional Court of the Queen's Bench Division hears appeals by way of case stated (i.e. on a point of law) from magistrates' courts and possibly, on occasion, the Crown Court.

The Court of Appeal (Criminal Division)
This court deals with appeals against convictions arrived at by a jury or sentences imposed by a judge at the Crown Court. It also deals with any references by the attorney-general with regard to unduly lenient sentences; and references to the Court of Appeal by the Criminal Cases Review Commission (CCRC). Under a modern innovation, it can also tender advice where requested to do so by the Sentencing Guidelines Council (SGC) – as it has been asked to do in relation to appropriate levels of sentence for possessing child pornography. The Court of Appeal is served by Lords Justices of Appeal although High Court judges may also sit there on occasion.

The House of Lords
As noted in the text, the House of Lords is not administered by HM Courts Service but by the Houses of Parliament. Historically and for some 600 years it has enjoyed a judicial function as well as a legislative one, the latter in its role as the upper house of Parliament. In its judicial role it has been the final court of appeal on points of law and its rulings are binding on all courts below it under the doctrine of precedent. In modern times only professional lawyer/judges, known as Law Lords, have performed the judicial function of the House of Lords; and the Appellate Jurisdiction Act 1876 was passed to govern how that House hears various types of appeal. Subsequent legislation has created a rage of standing orders and practice directions. The House does not hear criminal appeals from Scotland.

A party seeks leave to appeal by way of a petition. Petitions are referred to an Appeal Committee of three Law Lords. The Appeal Committee's decision to

---

[6] In certain limited situations, 'judge-alone' trials are possible as to which other works should be consulted.

allow or refuse a petition is made depending on whether the case involves a point of law of general public importance that ought to be considered by the House. The Appeal Committee may ask the other party (the respondent) for his or her observations on the petition, but at this stage the Law Lords work mainly on the basis of written submissions, without a personal hearing. From time to time there is an oral hearing at which submissions are heard about whether or not to grant leave to appeal. Exceptionally, the House of lords can hear an appeal directly from the High Court.

The Law Lords deal with around 350 applications for leave to appeal each year; and allow about 100. Since the 1876 Act, the judicial work of the House has been carried out only by legally qualified Lords of Appeal in Ordinary, commonly called 'Law Lords'. At one time the Lord Chancellor sometimes sat as a judge, but since the Constitutional Reform Act 2005 no longer can do so. There are 12 Law Lords. They are equivalent to supreme court judges in other countries and when the new UK Supreme Court comes into operation, the Law Lords will become the first justices of the Supreme Court. Law Lords are appointed by The Queen on the advice of the prime minister, usually from the ranks of the senior appeal court judges in each part of the UK. The first woman 'Law Lady', Baroness Hale of Richmond, was appointed in 2004.

Since 2005, Law Lords are no longer full members of the House and cannot speak and or vote in the chamber of the house. In practice they rarely did so before. In addition to their judicial work, law lords are often asked to chair major public inquiries. Modern-day topics of inquiry have included the events of 'Bloody Sunday' in Northern Ireland and the death of the MOD scientist Dr David Kelly.

Once a hearing has finished the Law Lords discuss the case, the junior Lord giving his or her opinion first. Judgement is always given at a sitting in the House. The Law Lords' speeches are called opinions and are the equivalent of a judge's reasoned judgment in the courts. They stopped reading out their opinions in full in 1963 and now just indicate briefly how they would dispose of the appeal, referring to the speech which they have prepared, copies of which are available to all parties. The full text is also posted at www.parliament.uk immediately after each judgment.

Civil courts
Apart from the House of Lords, which has both criminal and civil jurisdiction, the civil courts comprise:

- county courts under a 'district judge (county courts)' who sits to hear claims up to the value (normally) of £15,000 in such matters as contract or tort (civil wrongs such as negligence and nuisance that have caused loss to the 'plaintiff'/applicant);

- the family courts under either a district judge, circuit judge or High Court judge, depending on which tier of court is dealing with the matter, sit to deal with a range of matters concerning divorce and family breakdown, including ruling on disputes over family property and related matters as well as making orders in relation to children, i.e. about who it is they will live with following such a break-up and/or who will pay for their upbringing, education, etc. They also have powers relating to exclusion from the matrimonial or family home, e.g. where there has been domestic violence or other interference as between spouses, partners or in relation to children. There is also a magistrates' family proceedings court that has a jurisdiction broadly equivalent to that of the county court in family matters. Family panel magistrates sit to deal with such matters. In all such matters relating to children the courts are supported by the Children and Family Courts Advisory and Support Service (CAFCASS);
- the High Court which also has a Queen's Bench Division (in effect the civil division that deals with contract, tort, etc. and is also the umbrella for the Commercial Court and Admiralty Court); a Chancery Division (e.g. to deal with equity, trusts, contentious wills, probate, etc., revenue matters, bankruptcy, companies and patent (via a Patents Court)); and an Administrative Court which exercises a supervisory jurisdiction concerning the legality of the decisions and actions of lower courts, tribunals, ministers and public authorities; and
- the Court of Appeal (Civil Division) that mirrors the Criminal Division of that court (above) at this level to hear appeals from the High Court and (in certain instances) county courts in civil matters and also from tribunals.

The Coroners Court

Coroners are independent judicial officers who sit in their own courts to investigate violent, unnatural deaths or sudden deaths where the cause is unknown or contentious. They also investigate deaths in police or prison custody which are reported to coroners as a matter of course. The MOJ has indicated that it is committed to strengthening and improving this essentially local service. A draft Coroners Bill seeks to modernise the coroner service 'by providing a better service for bereaved people' within a national framework and 'making sure that investigations and inquests are more effective'.

The office of coroner has survived for over 800 years and there are around 140 different local jurisdictions (or 'districts') in England and Wales. Each coroner is expected to be available whenever required and, due to the number of cases dealt with, approaching 30 coroners operate on a full-time basis. The remainder are remunerated depending on the number of cases referred to them. They are barristers, solicitors or medical practitioners of not less than five years standing. They may be assisted by similarly qualified deputy coroners or 'assistant deputy coroners' who may act in their place when they are out of their district or are otherwise unable to deal with a death that has been reported to them.

Appendix IV *The Governance of Britain: Foreword, Executive Summary and Introduction*

Foreword by The Right Honourable Gordon Brown, Prime Minister and The Right Honourable Jack Straw, Secretary of State for Justice and Lord Chancellor.

Our constitutional arrangements fundamentally underpin how we function as a nation. The nature of the relationship the Government has with citizens, the credibility of our institutions, and the rights and responsibilities of citizens all determine the health of our democracy.

Without a shared national purpose, and a strong bond between people and government, we cannot meet the challenges of today's world – whether in guaranteeing security, delivering world class education and health services, building strong communities, or responding to the challenges of globalisation.

In Britain, our constitution has evolved organically to renew the relationship between government and citizen, and to respond to the challenges we have faced as a nation. It is from this constant evolution that we draw strength. In 1997 the Government embarked upon a major programme of constitutional change: power was devolved away from Westminster, fundamental rights were enshrined in the Human Rights Act, freedom of information was introduced and we completed the first stage towards a reformed House of Lords.

But today we want to go further. We want to forge a new relationship between government and citizen, and begin the journey towards a new constitutional settlement – a settlement that entrusts Parliament and the people with more power.

The proposals published in this Green Paper seek to address two fundamental questions: how should we hold power accountable, and how should we uphold and enhance the rights and responsibilities of the citizen?

The paper does not seek to set out a final blueprint for our constitutional settlement. It is the first step in a national conversation. As Prime Minister and Secretary of State for Justice, we hope that people throughout the country – and from all walks of life – will participate in this debate. We believe it is vital to our strength as a democracy.

Executive summary

The Government's vision and proposals for constitutional renewal are set out in this document. The document explores the rights and responsibilities that shape the relationships which the people of this country have with each other. It considers the relationship people have with the institutions of the state, at a local, regional and national level.

This document discusses how to modernise the role of the executive in our system of governance. It looks at options to make both the executive, and Parliament, more accountable to the people and to reinvigorate our democracy. Some of the reforms proposed will be taken forward immediately, and some in legislation in the next session of Parliament. Some represent the first step towards a final outcome of renewing trust in our democratic institutions.

As part of this, the Government wants to engage people around the country in a discussion on citizenship and British values and will be conducting a series of events around the UK to gain as much input as possible.

Limiting the powers of the executive

The Government will seek to surrender or limit powers which it considers should not, in a modern democracy, be exercised exclusively by the executive (subject to consultation with interested parties and, where necessary, legislation). These include powers to:

- deploy troops abroad;
- request the dissolution of Parliament;
- request the recall of Parliament;
- ratify international treaties without decision by Parliament;
- determine the rules governing entitlement to passports and for the granting of pardons;
- restrict parliamentary oversight of the intelligence services;
- choose bishops;
- have a say in the appointment of judges;
- direct prosecutors in individual criminal cases; and
- establish the rules governing the Civil Service.

The Government will also:

- work to increase parliamentary scrutiny of some public appointments, ensure that appointments are appropriately scrutinised more generally; and
- review the role of the Attorney General to ensure that the office retains the public's confidence.

Making the executive more accountable

The Government will act to ensure that it is answerable to Parliament and the people. The Government has published a revised Ministerial Code with new arrangements for independent advice to Ministers and more transparency around Ministers' interests and travel.

The Government will:

- consider legislation with the aim of maximising the effectiveness of the Intelligence and Security Committee and, in the interim, propose changes to improve the transparency and resourcing of the Committee;
- publish a National Security Strategy which will be overseen by a new National Security Committee, chaired by the Prime Minister;
- introduce a pre-Queen's Speech consultative process on its legislative programme;
- simplify the reporting of Government expenditure to Parliament;
- invite Parliament to hold annual parliamentary debates on the objectives and plans of major Government Departments; and
- limit the pre-release of official statistics to Ministers to 24 hours before publication.

Re-invigorating our democracy

The Government will:

- continue to develop reforms for a substantially or wholly elected second chamber;
- consider extending the duration in which parties can use all-women shortlists for the selection of electoral candidates;
- better enable local people to hold service providers to account;
- place a duty on public bodies to involve local people in major decisions;
- assess the merits of giving local communities the ability to apply for devolved or delegated budgets;

- consult on moving voting to weekends for general and local elections;
- complete and publish a review of voting systems in line with the Government's manifesto commitment; and
- review the provisions that govern the right to protest in the vicinity of Parliament.

Britain's future: the citizen and the state

The Government will:

- initiate an inclusive process of national debate to develop a British statement of values;
- work with Lord Goldsmith to conduct a review of British citizenship;
- launch a Youth Citizenship Commission, looking at citizenship education, ceremonies and the possibility of reducing the voting age; and
- consult on the current guidance on flying the Union Flag from government buildings and Westminster Parliament.

The Governance of Britain: Introduction

1. In every generation of our country's life, the relationship between the individual and the state, the rights and responsibilities of each and the role of our public institutions have been the subject of review, debate and reform.

2. Sometimes that reform has been evolutionary, with the gradual development of new ways of working and new relationships. Sometimes it has required a step change through legislation. Sometimes (although not for centuries) it has taken the form of revolution. But together, these reforms have developed our country from a feudal monarchy where the King's word was law and only a tiny minority had any real influence, to a representative democracy governed through a sovereign Parliament elected by universal suffrage. Alongside the growth of Parliament, we have seen the development of our common law, which for centuries has underpinned many of our most cherished rights and freedoms.

3. The pace of change has varied, but it has always been achieved through a process of discussion, and by combining an enduring respect for the value of tradition with a determination to change when change is needed … This Government is proud to play a key role in continuing this process of constitutional renewal. We have a responsibility to ensure that the values of this and future generations are reflected in the constitution and fabric of British politics and society.

4. Sometimes, the evolution of the constitution has failed to keep pace with the evolution of society, or government has been unwilling to recognise the need for reform, or an institution has been stretched so far that further evolutionary reform is impossible. In those circumstances, legislative intervention has proved necessary. And it is those landmark legislative reforms of which we think when looking at previous constitutional reform programmes.

5. The 20th century saw a large amount of change in society, economy and politics, which went beyond the ability of the constitution to cope with simply through adaptation or evolution. There was a significant degree of pressing demand for constitutional change.

6.   From 1997, the Labour Government began introducing the constitutional changes required in a modern democracy. These included:

- creating a Scottish Parliament and Welsh Assembly, and making devolution a practical reality;
- modernisation of the House of Lords, ending the right of the majority of hereditary peers to be members of the House;
- establishing the independence of the Bank of England, allowing interest rate decisions to be made free of active political involvement;
- embedding a modern Human Rights Act into United Kingdom law, giving the domestic courts the ability to rule on human rights issues;
- introducing the Freedom of Information Act, increasing transparency and the ability to hold Government to account;
- reforming the role of Lord Chancellor so that the holder of the office is no longer head of the judiciary or Speaker of the House of Lords;
- legislating to create a new free-standing Supreme Court, separating the highest appeal court from Parliament and removing the Law Lords from the legislature;
- establishing an independent Judicial Appointments Commission to select candidates for judicial office;
- establishing a new system of devolved government in London with the creation of the Greater London Authority; and
- establishing the Northern Ireland Assembly, providing the opportunity for a continued, stable settlement for the first time in generations.

7.   The Government is proud of these achievements. But we must go further if we are to meet the challenges which remain:

- power remains too centralised and too concentrated in government;
- it is not sufficiently clear what power government should and should not have;
- some people have become cynical about, and increasingly disengaged from, the political process;[7] and

---

[7] Surveys consistently display very low levels of trust in politicians. In 1983, 18 per cent of people trusted politicians to tell the truth. This fell to a low of just 15 per cent in 1997 before rising to 20 per cent in 2005. Source: Ipsos MORI, *Opinion of Professions*, survey of c.2000 British adults aged 15 years plus. Available at http://www.ipsos-mori.com/polls/trends/truth.shtml

- Britain needs to articulate better a shared understanding of what it means to be British, and of what it means to live in the UK.

8. The time has come to build a consensus about the changes that we can make together to help renew trust and confidence in our democratic institutions, to make them fit for the modern world and to begin properly to articulate and celebrate what it means to be British. Renewing the fabric of our nation is not a one-off project or some meaningless side-show. The aim of the proposals in this paper should be to create a renewed bond between government and the people it serves, bringing people closer to the decision-making process at both the local and national level. By rebalancing some aspects of the way power is exercised, the Government hopes to ensure that individual citizens feel more closely engaged with those representing them; able to have their voice heard, active in their communities and bound together by common ties.

9. The Government intends to initiate an inclusive national debate through which the whole country can come together to develop a British statement of values. This national debate will provide an opportunity to begin exploring the wider issue of citizenship and the future of our constitutional arrangements which underpin everything about how we function as a nation.

10. The Government has these goals:

- to invigorate our democracy, with people proud to participate in decision-making at every level;
- to clarify the role of government, both central and local;
- to rebalance power between Parliament and the Government, and give Parliament more ability to hold the Government to account; and
- to work with the British people to achieve a stronger sense of what it means to be British, and to launch an inclusive debate on the future of the country's constitution.

11. Only a confident UK will be able to adapt to the economic challenges of globalisation. Only a country sure of its identity will be able to come together to ensure our mutual security: common, inclusive values can help us overcome the threat from extremism of all kinds. Only a nation certain of its national purpose will be able to pull together to meet the common challenges of global climate change. And only by coming

together as a diverse country and debating our common values, our citizenship and our constitution can we begin to forge the sense of purpose and renew the common bonds that will allow us to meet these challenges together.

Next steps

12. This document sets out a range of proposals that the Government believes will meet its objectives. Some will be introduced through legislation in the next session of Parliament. Some represent the start of a process of consultation, and over the coming weeks and months the Government will conduct various discussions in various ways to ensure that the proposals contained here can be best effected.

13. Some of the ideas and measures proposed will apply to the whole of the United Kingdom. But the devolution settlement means that some issues are in the hands of the devolved legislatures of Scotland, Wales and Northern Ireland. The Government's proposals in those cases apply only in England but it hopes that the devolved administrations will be equally involved in the dialogue to come.

Appendix V *Some Further Reading and Internet Sources*

There is remarkably little in the way of a direct account of the history of the Ministry of Justice (MOJ) in its former incarnation as the Department of Constitutional Affairs (DCA) or earlier as the Lord Chancellor's Department (LCD). There is, to be sure, a good deal on the constitution or constitutional principle, including the classic texts of AV Dicey, *Introduction to the Study of the Law of the Constitution* (1885), and Walter Bagehot, *The English Constitution* (1867), alluded to in *Chapter 6*. Similarly, there are ample texts, e.g. on the courts of law, prisons and probation matters or even on victims and witnesses, not least, e.g. Martin Wright's *Justice for Victims and Offenders: A Restorative Response to Crime* (1996), Waterside Press. Some background concerning the Lord Chancellor's Department can be found in Sir Thomas Skyrme's voluminous, *The History of the Justice of the Peace* (1986), Barry Rose as there is in Professor Jackson's *The Machinery of Justice in England* (1940), Jackson R M, Cambridge University Press.

But in general there is as likely to be as much if not more atmosphere in Gilbert and Sullivan's musical offerings as there is in the library archives. A J Burgesses ornate limited edition, *The Notary and other Lawyers in Gilbert and Sullivan* (1997), contains many references and portraits and drawings of Lord Chancellors as well as a chapter analysing the role of the Lord Chancellor in *Iolanthe*. Maybe it is, or was, the somewhat secretive and obscure nature of the LCD, originally and pre-Second World War more in the nature of a set of barristers' chambers, that accounts for this reticence to put pen to paper. Matters may well only have begun to see the light of day after the LCD took over the Court Service in the 1970s upon the abolition of the sometimes equally perplexing Assizes and Quarter Sessions. We now live in a different era, one of scrutiny, openness, transparency and freedom of information and hopefully this is something that is now well on the way to being corrected.

Other references to the Lord Chancellor and occasionally the LCD are to be found in legal biographies and autobiographies such as those of Lord Birkenhead, e.g. *F E Smith: First Earl of Birkenhead* (1983) by John Campbell, Jonathan Cape, *Richard Burdon Haldane: An Autobiography* (1929) by Viscount Haldane himself (naturally). In contrast, Lord Hailsham devotes just a few pages to his time on the Woolsack in an otherwise lengthy autobiography *A Sparrow's Flight* (1991), Hogg Q, HarperCollins - despite his relatively long time as Lord Chancellor, preferring, it seems, to concentrate on the more overtly political aspects of his career. Indeed, this may be indicative: many Lords Chancellors may have hoped for 'better things' rather than being asked to undertake no greater responsibility than that of upholding the constitution and keeping the judges in order! John Hostettler has written of Lord Halsbury who edited *The Laws of England* as an adjunct to his office (*Lord Halsbury* (1998), Barry Rose).

Anthony Mockler wrote a book, *Lions Under the Throne. A History of the Lord Chief Justices of England* (1983), Frederick Muller Limited. Whilst not about Lords Chancellors per se, it does contain a number of passages in which individual Lord Chancellors were at odds with the Lord Chief Justice of the Day, which might prove instructive in any modern-day conflict.

David Faulkner's acclaimed work, *Crime State and Citizen: A Field Full of Folk* published in 2001 and in a second edition with a Foreword by Rod Morgan in 2006 (both Waterside Press) is mentioned in the text. There is perhaps no better work for anyone seeking to get to grips with issues of governance that lie behind the developments of 2007 – and the creation of the MOJ - than to study that book.

Some background information is to be found by searching on the internet, e.g. at www.nationalarchives.gov.uk, whilst for modern-day information there is no better place to start than at www.justice.gov.uk the new MOJ web-site that has links to many of the topics mentioned in the chapters of this book. A good number of individual web-site address also appear in the main text or the footnotes of this book.

Index